Towards Fifth-Generation Computers

G L Simons

PUBLISHED BY NCC PUBLICATIONS

British Library Cataloguing in Publication Data

Simons, G. L.
 Towards fifth-generation computers.
 1. Electronic digital computers
 I. Title
 001.64   QA76.5

 ISBN 0-85012-390-9

First published in 1983 by:
NCC Publications, The National Computing Centre Limited, Oxford Road, Manchester M1 7ED, England.

Typeset in 11pt Times Roman and printed in England by UPS Blackburn Limited, 76-80 Northgate, Blackburn, Lancashire.

ISBN 0-85012-390-9

Acknowledgements

The information in this book is largely derived from journal articles, brochures, conference proceedings and books. Most of these are listed in the bibliography (Appendix 1). I am grateful to the following people for making relevant material available to me:

David Fairbairn, Director, NCC
Derek Scriven, Group Director, NCC
John Pritchard, Senior Consultant, NCC

I am also grateful to Malcolm Peltu for lending me crucial material, and I have also drawn on the neatly encapsulated historical and other items in his excellent *Introducing Computers* (NCC Publications, 1983). I am grateful to Alex d'Agapeyeff for indicating some sources of useful information: his *Expert Systems, Fifth Generation and UK Suppliers* (NCC Publications, 1983) proved to be helpful background reading.

Thanks are due to the Japan Information Processing and Development Centre (JIPDEC) for permission to reproduce particular drawings that appeared in the *Proceedings of the International Conference on Fifth-Generation Computer Systems* (1981). This publication provided invaluable information about the Japanese fifth-generation concepts and research plans. Thanks are also due to Logica for providing information about the Logos speech recognition system, and for permission to use the Logos functional diagram (Chapter 5).

NCC staff helped in various ways. I am grateful to Janice Wooding and Anne Johnson (both of NCC Publications) for helping with research and for checking the material at various stages. Thanks are also due to Roger Brady (Head of Information Division) for sending me useful books and for making information available for research.

Geoff Simons
Chief Editor

Introduction

This is an introductory book. Its central purpose is to draw attention to the main trends and developments that will together contribute to the birth of *fifth-generation computers*. This means that
many topics are considered – from non-silicon integrated circuits
to new programming languages, from cognitive psychology to
modern 'expert' systems, from voice recognition to visual perception in machines.

It is inevitable that, with such a plethora of crucial and insistent
topics, the treatment is relatively superficial (though readers are
led to more detailed sources). Again and again, in order to keep
the book to a reasonable size I resisted the temptation to explore
this topic or that in more depth, to expand brief sections to whole
chapters, to indulge personal interest in particular subject areas.
The aim has been to survey a spectrum of relevant topics in a
balanced and economical way.

Chapter 1 profiles the background to the fifth-generation programme, highlighting the historical evolution of computer systems,
defining the identifiable 'generations' of computers, and drawing
attention to some of the converging trends that are influencing the
emergence of new-generation systems. In Chapter 2, the character
of fifth-generation computers is explored with reference to system
features, architectures, software and other aspects. Attention is
also given to the clear social requirements, as seen by the Japanese,
that fifth-generation systems will be designed to meet.

The broad research goal is to develop computers that are more
powerful, more flexible, more competent, more intelligent . . .

Chapters 3 to 5 describe the main contributing elements to this goal. Various aspects of *artificial intelligence* (AI) are profiled in Chapter 3 as relevant to the character of new-generation systems. Problem-solving and inference-making, central to fifth-generation computers, have been researched in AI for many years: these functions and others are explored as relevant to the character of new-generation computers. Particular attention is given to the nature of *expert systems* (Chapter 4) – how they are configured as knowledge-processing facilities, the character of expert-system software, and potential and actual applications areas. Expert systems, usually with conversational and inference-making abilities, are generally regarded as a principal contributing element in fifth-generation development. And attention is also given (in Chapter 5) to the requirements of increased 'user friendliness', the nature of the emerging *intelligent man/machine interface*. Here a profile is given of developments in such AI areas as natural-language understanding, voice recognition, speech synthesis and machine vision.

Chapter 6 highlights particular features of the international response to fifth-generation computers. A principal UK response was the setting up of the Alvey committee. We focus on the subsequent report and on the response (or lack of it) that it has generated in the UK computer industry and the UK Government. At the time (February 1983) this book went to press, there were reports that the UK Department of Industry had approved the £350m funding (over five years) requested by the Alvey Committee, and that firm Government approval would follow after consultation with other Departments.

Finally, Chapter 7 draws attention to developments in three areas – synergetics, biochips and robotics – to illustrate how disparate trends will influence the theory and practice of tomorrow's computers. This highlights what is perhaps the central feature of modern computer development: the phenomenon of *convergence,* emphasised in the present book.

Many disciplines and technologies – integrated circuit fabrication, biology, software engineering, psychology, knowledge-representation methods, artificial intelligence, communications techniques, new formalised reasoning methods (eg 'fuzzy' logic), sensor engineering, etc – are combining to yield the new generation of computers. Clearly, a fifth generation of computers will emerge, but until it does, we cannot be sure how it will look. We know its parentage in existing computers and in the concepts of human researchers, but computer evolution is so rapid and so multifaceted that we cannot predict its future course with certainty.

The broad movement *towards fifth-generation computers* could be described in a thousand books. The present volume is intended to give a flavour of what is happening, a few insights into the most ambitious programme yet witnessed by the international computer industry.

Contents

1 Background

INTRODUCTION

Computer systems are evolving at a rapid rate: we have learned not to be surprised at the remarkable pace of technological development in this field. Changes in one area (say semiconductor integration technology) stimulate the possibility of change in others (say, problem-solving methods or speech synthesis). Developments in software (such as logic programming) affect the competence of computer systems intended to perform intelligent tasks (such as making decisions or drawing inferences). And the various converging developments enhance the scope for effective applications – in fields ranging from geological prospecting to home information systems, from medical diagnosis to industrial robotics, from biochemical analysis to product design.

Practical electronic computing has existed for only about four decades, though contributing ideas have been formulated over a period of more than two thousand years (see History of Computing, below). During its relatively brief existence the working computer, like other artefacts and living creatures, has moved through several generations. To some extent these have been recognised with hindsight: developments, mainly in semiconductor technology, laid the basis for new families of computers which came to define the shape and character of new computer generations. Though new generations of computers were envisaged, there were – until the late-1970s – few attempts to chart in detail the route whereby an ambitious new computer generation could be developed and implemented.

It is perhaps a unique feature of the fifth generation of computers that its character is so comprehensively defined in advance (see Chapter 2).

For fifth generation, research goals for hardware and software are being formulated; likely computer languages and system architectures have been (or are being) identified; and specific applications possibilities – to a large extent deriving from current working systems in such areas as medical diagnosis and factory automation – are being explored. Timescales for particular research and implementation goals are being formulated.

The four preceding computer generations (see below) have been defined with varying degrees of precision and coherency, but only the fifth generation has been so heralded in the media, so clearly prefigured in research programmes, so widely anticipated by pundits, politicians and computer specialists alike. And it is clearly conceivable, however unlikely, that the fifth generation, at least in its currently defined shape, will never emerge (there is, for example, debate about the success of several years' development of expert systems). After all, there is no precedent to the present situation: never before has such a technologically ambitious outcome been predicted with so many problems waiting to be solved (for example, equipping *computers* with 'knowledge' as opposed to 'data' is likely to require a greatly increased understanding of *human* cognitive processes – see Chapters 3 and 4).

The predicted birth of fifth generation is contingent upon a successful outcome to hundreds of different research programmes. There can be little doubt that much will be achieved, but will it all amount to Fifth Generation as currently conceived?

This chapter outlines the background to fifth-generation computer systems, providing some historical information, indicating landmark dates, and profiling also the first four computer generations. A brief indication, expanded in later chapters, is also given of how several disparate trends and developments – in such areas as semiconductor technology, expert systems and artificial intelligence (AI) – are contributing to the ambitious concept of fifth-generation configurations. Finally, an indication is given of the role of Japan as virtual initiator of the broad fifth-generation programme.

HISTORY OF COMPUTING

The history of any technology is a complex mix of *fantasy, theory* and *practicality*. This is true of computers and robots as it is true of genetic engineering and aerospace technology. Hephaestus (*Iliad,* Book XVIII) devised golden maidens 'filled with minds and wisdom', evident precursors of modern domestic and industrial robots, but there is no indication that Homer had any insight into the theoretical principles from which the modern science of robotics would derive. Aristotle, by contrast, in analysing syllogistic form more than two thousand years ago, began the science of logic which would yield a secure theoretical basis for the organisation of circuits in the modern electronic computer.

In practical terms, the first types of mechanical calculating devices, the various versions of the *abacus,* were developed to aid the activities of the engineers, mathematicians and traders of the Ancient World. In China and Japan, thousands of years B.C., the abacus took the form of beads on a special frame (the beads becoming known as *calculi,* the origin of the word *calculate*). A typical abacus carried beads threaded in columns, with the positions of beads representing digits. (This is analogous to how electronic computers came to store information in punched cards and paper tape: the absence or presence of holes in particular positions, taken together, represented the required numerical quantities.)

A further important development in mechanical calculators was the Arithmetic Engine produced by Blaise Pascal in 1647. This device, called the Pascaline, worked on a similar principle to mechanical milometers (or 'hodometers', known in the Ancient Greco-Roman world). Here digits from 0 to 9 were arranged on wheels: when a wheel was turned one full revolution, its neighbour was caused to be advanced by one notch. As with the construction of later mechanical calculating devices, difficulties were experienced in the manufacture of reliable components.

In 1666, Sir Samuel Morland produced an adding and subtracting machine similar to the Pascaline (Samuel Pepys commented: 'Very pretty but not very useful.'); and in 1673 the Morland multiplying calculator was introduced. At about the same time,

Leibniz in Germany had developed an effective calculator to perform multiplication and division, this device exploiting the idea of a stepped wheel with teeth of nine different lengths to represent the ten digits. The required calculations were performed by the interaction of the wheels. Leibniz, impressed with the simplicity of binary arithmetic, considered using binary in a mechanical calculator, though it was 150 years later before algebra – at the hands of such mathematicians as Boole and de Morgan – was developed to the point at which binary notation could serve as a powerful computing facility.

Charles Babbage, born in 1792 and who contrived two of the most ambitious mechanical calculating machines, is often represented as the 'father of modern computing'. His first machine was presented to the Royal Astronomical Society in 1821. Using a technique based on calculating the differences between numbers, it was called the *Difference Engine*. A main purpose was to compute and check mathematical tables. In a simple version the Engine worked to six decimal places but production problems proved too difficult for a larger, more complicated machine. However, in 1859 a model was built to prepare life tables for insurance companies in calculating premiums. (In 1926, Dr L J Crombie at the British Nautical Almanac began work to automate calculation of the positions of the sun and stars, the task for which Babbage had designed his machine. Crombie realised that a particular Burroughs accounting machine could be used without modification as a Difference Engine.)

By the early-1830s, Babbage realised the limitations of the device: in particular, it had been constructed to perform one specific task and would require total re-engineering to carry out other types of calculation. With this in mind, he began the design of a *general-purpose computing machine,* the Analytical Engine. In developing this device, he seems to have provided no single coherent description of the machine (he was evidently poor on documentation!). The best account we have is largely due to Ada Lovelace, Babbage's co-worker for many years.

Following a Babbage lecture in Turin, a young Italian military engineer, L. F. Menabrea, wrote an account of the machine in French (published in 1842). Lovelace translated the paper into

English, whereupon Babbage encouraged her to write many detailed additions of her own. These additions included programs which she had discussed with Babbage and which, with one exception, she had originated. She also discovered 'a grave mistake' in Babbage's proposal for calculating Bernoulli numbers – perhaps the first recorded example of a program bug. The Menabrea paper was expanded by Lovelace to three times its original length, and Babbage was delighted by this clear demonstration of the power of the Analytical Engine.

The importance of this machine consisted in how it defined the elements essential to any general-purpose computer system. Long before the emergence of modern electronics technology, Babbage realised that computers would have to include five key elements or facilities:

— *input,* to allow numbers to be fed into the machine. Babbage used the punched cards originally developed by Jacquard for the automatic control of looms. Cards were still used for computer input well into the 1970s;

— *store,* to be used as a memory for the numbers used in calculations and for the program instructions. For this purpose, Babbage considered using punched cards and metal disks on spindles;

— *arithmetic unit,* to perform the actual calculations. Babbage called this the *mill* ('mill time' is still used, though not commonly, to denote the time spent by a program in processing activities);

— *control unit,* to control task performance under the direction of the stored program. Today the arithmetic unit and the control unit are usually combined to form the central processing unit (CPU);

— *output,* to communicate to users the results of processing. Babbage considered using punched cards and setting up type automatically to give printed output.

The designs and programs formulated by Babbage and Lovelace achieved little in practical terms: it was about 100 years before a means was found of building such a machine reliably and economically. But it is hard to over-estimate the theoretical importance of this work. Writing of mankind Babbage commented in 1851: 'His earliest contrivances to support uncivilised life were tools of the simplest and rudest construction. His latest achievements in the substitution of machinery, not merely for the skill of the human hand, but for the relief of the human intellect, are founded on the use of tools of a still higher order'.

After Babbage, Dr Herman Hollerith – who won a competition to find an efficient way of analysing the 1890 American census – was perhaps the next landmark figure. He too made use of the Jacquard card as an input medium. Holes (or their absence) in particular positions on the cards signalled particular characteristics about the individuals in the census. To read the cards, rods were passed through them to make contact with a bowl of mercury to make an electrical contact to cause a counter to advance by one. The Hollerith tabulator was therefore the first computing machine to employ non-mechanical processing means, a highly successful approach that was exploited by a company that became known as International Business Machines (IBM), the largest computer manufacturer in the world.

For the first forty years of the Twentieth Century there were few dramatic innovations in computer technology. In 1892, William Burroughs had introduced the first commercially-available adding machine, and a variety of tabulators, adding machines and comptometers remained in widespread use until commercial electronic computers began to make an impact in the 1960s. By the early-1940s it proved possible, following the work of Vannevar Bush with thermionic valves, to use such electronic components as elements in digital computing circuits. The scene was set for the rapid development of modern electronic computing.

In 1935, Konrad Zuse introduced binary operations into an entirely mechanical machine, the Z1. The next model (Z2) used electromechanical relays instead of mechanical switches and employed punched paper tape as input. Later models were also based on relays. (The Zuse computer company was bought by Siemens in 1969.) A project funded by IBM yielded in 1943 the Harvard Mark 1, again based on electromagnetic relays. And in the same year the Colossus 1, the first electronic computer, went into operation in Britain to decipher the messages produced by Enigma, a German code generator. Two thousand thermionic valves were used in Colossus, specifically designed for this cryptographic application.

The Second World War also stimulated the work of Dr John Mauchly and J. Presper Eckert (of the Moore School of Electrical Engineering at the University of Pennsylvania). The aim was to build a machine, eventually called Electronic Numerical Integrator and Calculator (ENIAC), to carry out the rapid calculations needed to compile ballistics tables for guns and missiles. ENIAC went into operation in 1946, comprising 18,000 valves but only able to store twenty 10-digit numbers. The machine, like Colossus, was a special-purpose device: it could be reprogrammed but only with laborious effort, a manifest disadvantage.

In June 1945, John von Neumann embarked upon the design of a new machine, the Electronic Discrete Variable Automatic Computer (EDVAC). The publication of the ensuing report proved to be a turning point in computer developments, though EDVAC was not built until the early-1950s. For the first time, the concept of *stored-program control* had been incorporated into the design of an electronic digital computer. The first operational computer of this type was the Manchester Automatic Digital Machine, usually known as the Manchester University Mark 1. This computer ran its first program in June 1948, and three versions of the machine were commissioned between 1948 and 1949. By October 1949, various enhancements had been added to the original Mark 1 specification, including:

— extended order-code including a peripheral control order for programmed drum transfers and input/output transfers;

— provision of input/output routines using 5-bit teleprinter code and paper tape devices.

This machine was used in various ways in 1949/50, including investigating the Riemann hypothesis and making various types of calculations in optics. It was closed down in 1950, by which time Ferranti had almost completed manufacture of the first production Mark 1 (the development of the Mark 1 and subsequent events are well described by Lavington, 1975).

In 1947, Maurice Wilkes and a team from Cambridge began construction of the Electronic Delay Storage Automatic Computer (EDSAC), and in May 1949 the system carried out its first fully-automatic calculation. Here a key innovation was the software strategy, involving the development of programming concepts such as standard subroutines to perform frequently-required calculations and aids to help find program errors. EDSAC also featured the first computer *operating* system, ie software that organises the machine's resources to satisfy the needs of the various programs.

The development of computer technology accelerated in the 1950s, with commercial companies taking up many of the prototypes emerging from the university laboratories. For example, the Ferranti Mark 1 became operational in February 1951, shortly before one of the best known early commercial computers, the Lyons Electronic Office (LEO). Manchester University went on to design a number of other machines, including the Ferranti Mercury in 1957 and the Ferranti Atlas (its first user service became available in 1963). The transistor, invented in 1948 at the Bell Telephone Laboratories, had by now replaced the original thermionic valves: computer circuits were smaller, more reliable, and required less energy to operate. The first stage in the progressive miniaturisation of data processing power was now complete.

The large *mainframe* computers continued to dominate commercial computing through the 1960s, though, aided by transistor developments, new popular families of small computers *(minicomputers)* were beginning to emerge. The PDP-8, from Digital Equipment Corporation (DEC) was the first really popular minicomputer. By the 1970s, with the development of integrated circuits, it was clear that computers would become smaller and more powerful. In the late-1960s, thousands of transistor elements were assembled on minute chips of silicon: where ENIAC had weighed more than 30 tons and required a room 60 ft by 25 ft to hold it, a computer of superior capability could, by 1971, be accommodated on a sliver of silicon the size of a thumb-nail.

The first microprocessor (a complete computer CPU), produced by Intel Corporation in 1971, was based on a single $\frac{1}{4}$-inch-square silicon chip which carried the equivalent of 2250 transistors, all the computer circuitry necessary for an arithmetic and control unit. By 1976, chips of this size could carry more than 20,000 components. Today, in 1983, there is talk of fabricating one million electronic components – transistors, capacitors, diodes, etc – on a single silicon chip.

The most dramatic developments in computer technology over the last three decades have derived from advances in microelectronics: computers have become smaller, more reliable, and cheaper – and so increasingly within the reach of organisations and domestic users. Computer architectures have evolved less than the supporting fabrication technologies: the block diagram of an early valve-based computer is surprisingly similar to that of a modern microcomputer. With the emergence of fifth-generation systems we may expect rapid architectural evolution (eg away from CPU-focused von Neumann modes of processing) as well as rapid changes in microelectronics technologies (eg trends away from silicon towards gallium arsenide and other substances). The history of computing is marked by a series of significant innovations (some are listed in Table 1). We may expect more of these in the 1980s and 1990s as the fifth-generation research programmes bear fruit.

SUPERCOMPUTERS

It is worth saying something about supercomputers since they are sometimes identified with fifth-generation systems. In fact the term 'supercomputer' is variously used to denote the biggest or fastest computers currently available or alternatively the advanced systems 'just around the corner'. The earliest electronic computers – Colossus, ENIAC, EDVAC, etc – were regarded as 'super' computers when compared with the earlier mechanical and electromechanical devices; and in later years every new technological advance was seen to yield new 'super' systems. Today, supercom-

Date	Source	Innovation	Comment
1642	Pascal	calculating machine (Pascaline)	'I submit . . . a small machine . . . by means of which . . . you may perform all the operations of arithmetic...'
1694	von Leibniz	calculating machine	tried also to devise an algebra for logic
1770	Jacobson	calculating machine	able to compute numbers up to five digits
1801	Jacquard	automatic loom	use made of punched cards
1823	Babbage	Difference Engine	Lovelace: '... the Analytical Engine weaves algebraic patterns just as the Jacquard loom weaves flowers and leaves.'
1833-71	Babbage	Analytical Engine	
1854	Boole	algebra for logic	later universally adopted for computer use
1866	Hollerith	punch-card system	computer using electrical currents
1930	Bush	differential analyser	analogue computer for differential equations
1935	Zuse	mechanical Z1	use made of binary operations
1936	Turing	Turing 'machine'	theoretical system for computation
1938	Shannon	binary switching circuits	analysis of relay switching circuits
1943	Bletchley, England	Colossus 1	first electronic computer
1943	Harvard	Mark 1	use made of electromagnetic relays
1943-6	Eckert, Mauchly	ENIAC	electronic computer (5000 additions/second)
1947	von Neumann	EDVAC	turning point in computer design
1948	Manchester	Mark 1	later commercial production by Ferranti
1948	Bell Laboratories	transistor	basis of second-generation computers
1949	Cambridge	EDSAC	software innovations (eg operating system)
1954-7	NCR	NCR 304	first transistorised computer
1956	Dartmouth College	'artificial intelligence'	AI to become central in fifth generation
1957	Newell, Shaw, Simon	General Problem Solver	basis for important AI development
1960	DEC	PDP 8	first minicomputer
1971	Intel	microprocessor	crucial development for microelectronics
1972	Unimation	industrial robots	first company solely making robots
1979	Japan	5th-generation plans	programme for development first outlined
1991?	Japan, Europe, US?	first 5th-generation systems?	will achieved systems be truly 5th-generation?

Table 1   Milestones on the Road to Fifth-Generation Systems

puters, when they are not regarded as emerging fifth-generation systems, are usually taken to be computers from the CDC Cyber 205 family or from the Cray organisation.

At the same time there are various ways of approaching a functional definition of supercomputers. Spennewyn (1982) has quoted Frank Sumner, Barclays Professor of Microprocessor Applications in Industry at Manchester University: 'In 1979 supercomputer meant "super" in terms of the number of million floating operations performed a second (mflops). Nowadays systems are being discussed which merit the "super" in terms of facilities offered to the user, or in their capacity for highly-specialised data processing'. It is emphasised that some applications require vast amounts of computing power: for example, such applications as pattern recognition and knowledge-based (expert) systems. (Sumner: 'Array processors seem to be ideally suited to the first area and the major thrust of the Japanese Fifth Generation Project is to produce supercomputers for the second area.')

By 1980, very few supercomputers had been delivered to users, but by 1983 it was clear that international competition in this area had intensified. US computer specialists were emphasising the need for a national research and development programme in response to Japanese plans, in addition to the Fifth Generation scheme, for a $100m effort to build the world's largest computer. There is still only limited demand for the largest computers, which can cost around £6.5m (in early-1983) for applications in such areas as defence research, geological exploration and weather forecasting.

Cray has sold about fifty supercomputers, Control Data about twenty. However, such Japanese firms as Hitachi and Fujitsu are pressing hard. Hitachi has introduced the HAP-1 system and Fujitsu is marketing two machines, the VP100 and VP200, which at the same price as the CRAY X-MP are 20 per cent faster. Fujitsu aims to sell around eighty of these machines over the next five years. Control Data launched a four-pipeline version of the Cyber 205, rated at 800 megaflops, in late-1982, but there are rumours of a much superior machine about to emerge from Nippon Electric.

One approach to supercomputer design is to provide enhanced

scope for parallel operation. Dual-processor computers were followed, in the late-1970s, by systems (eg the CRAY1) containing as many as sixteen processors and able to execute up to one hundred million instructions per second (compare this with ENIAC's 5000 additions per second). But there are problems in simply increasing the number of parallel processors: for example, inevitable processing delays occur through the need for the various programs to communicate with each other. What we are now seeing is a move away from traditional computer architectures to overcome the anticipated shortfall in computer performance for necessary applications over the next few years. This development will be a key element in fifth-generation research.

Supercomputers using *data flow architectures* have been built in a number of universities and by some manufacturers. This approach abandons the idea, common in traditional von Neumann designs, that program instructions have to be obeyed in a fixed sequential manner. Here, any instructions can be obeyed when relevant data is available for processing. A communications network is employed to channel particular instructions to instruction queues associated with individual processors. In this way the computer can arrange for instructions to be obeyed irrespective of their position in the program. Data flow computers configured on this basis can simultaneously handle as many as five hundred processors, allowing, in principle, up to one billion instructions to be performed every second. Data flow architectures are likely to feature strongly in systems research intended to contribute to the emergence of fifth-generation computers. And this has far-reaching hardware and software implications: network designs will need to keep communication delays to a minimum, and there will be a growing requirement for computer languages that are not prejudiced in favour of traditional von Neumann architectures.

It is clear that supercomputers are recognised in part according to acknowledged performance criteria and in part according to their relationship to specific ambitious research programmes for fifth-generation and other advanced systems. Some specific fifth-generation functions (eg those associated with aspects of artificial intelligence) require greatly-enhanced processing power, and this feature is seen as a common characteristic of supercomputers. What this implies is that, in one sense, fifth-generation research has been underway for many years: researchers in this area will continue to explore possible hardware and software innovations which in the past were not specifically dubbed 'fifth-generation'. This simple semantic point may be taken as signalling the convergence of many computing trends (see below) which were running long before the first heady fifth-generation declarations of the late-1970s. It seems likely that we would have moved rapidly – via new architectures, new software, the need for user-friendly (and user-helpful) systems, etc – towards fifth-generation-type systems, even if we had been less self-conscious about the process.

COMPUTER GENERATIONS

It is now possible to define the first four generations of computers. These have been characterised in various ways but most commonly in terms of the technology of their hardware.

The *first generation* of computers (eg such machines as EDSAC and Colossus) were built out of thermionic valves. Systems were cumbersome, unreliable and needed ancillary cooling equipment to cope with the heat generated. Various software developments (eg the operating system in EDSAC) were introduced during this phase.

Second-generation computers (eg IBM 1401 and NCR 304) were built out of transistors, following the pioneering work (late 1940s) of William Shockley, John Bardeen and Walter Brattain at the Bell Telephone Laboratories in the US.

Third-generation computers (eg IBM S/360 and ICL 1900) were built out of integrated circuits: transistors, resistors, capacitors and diodes were effectively fabricated in a 10-μm-thick surface layer on a silicon wafer. The components were then connected by a metal layer evaporated onto the silicon, subsequent etching producing the required interconnections. By now, high-level programming languages (eg COBOL and FORTRAN) and sophisticated operating systems (eg IBM OS and ICL George 3) were well established.

Fourth-generation computers (eg IBM 3081 and Fujitsu M380) are characterised by enhanced levels of circuit integration through VLSI (very large-scale integration) techniques. Various software and architectural innovations have been introduced during this phase.

Fifth-generation computers (with 1991 set as a target date for a prototype machine) will have a number of features:

—   new advanced fabrication technologies, possibly based on substances other than silicon;

—   trend away from traditional high-level languages (such as FORTRAN and COBOL) towards languages with enhanced symbol manipulating and logic programming facilities (eg such languages as PROLOG and LISP);

—   emphasis on new (eg data flow) architectures (ie away from traditional von Neumann configurations);

—   new 'user-friendly' input/output methods (eg voice recognition, pattern recognition, speech synthesis, natural language processing) (see Chapters 3 and 5);

—   artificial intelligence (eg problem-solving, inference-making, knowledge-handling capabilities). Features in this area will be closely associated with research into expert systems (see Chapters 3 and 4).

A key element in the evolution towards fifth-generation systems is the convergence of many formerly disparate trends. It is worth highlighting these before considering various fifth-generation features in more detail. An effective fifth-generation computer will be a highly complex knowledge-processing system: the successful birth of such a system will depend upon many different disciplines and technologies.

CONVERGENCE OF TRENDS

General

The complexity of anticipated fifth-generation configurations derives largely from the ambitious character of the development programme. For example, expert systems, intimately related to fifth-generation plans, require new approaches to software and to data storage; artificial intelligence, not yet a mature discipline, is likely to benefit from new insights into human cognitive processes;

and the 'user-friendly' requirement in fifth generation demands a rapid development in such areas as speech understanding and natural language processing. The successful emergence of true fifth-generation computers will depend upon real progress in these and other fields. And underlying the specific data manipulation and functional requirements are the fabrication technologies needed to support the necessary rates and reliability of processing. Traditionally, following first-generation systems, electronic data processing has relied upon the features of semiconductors and integrated circuits.

Integrated Circuits

Silicon technology is likely to remain the dominant computer component technology in the near future despite, for example, IBM research into Josephson-junction devices and experiments with new substrate materials. W. Anacker has observed (in *IBM Journal of Research and Development,* March 1980) that 'Josephson computer technology provides excellent potential for ultra-high-performance computer mainframes complete with processors and memories hierarchies'. The new range of processor cycle times, even used with current computer architectures, 'could provide mainframes with 10- to 100-fold higher computing rates than that of an IBM 3033 mainframe system'. Josephson devices are seen as having fast switching properties, low power dissipation and other characteristics that are important in the development of high-performance computers. At the same time, cost will influence the adoption of new fabrication technologies and it is acknowledged that the silicon-based approach is currently the only technology capable of very large-scale integration (VLSI) in a cost-effective form.

Research into fabrication technologies focuses both on improving silicon-based circuits and on experimenting with new elements and compounds. As circuit miniaturisation is developed, a variety of problems can arise. For example, in extending C-MOS processes to 1μm or finer grain geometries, there can occur a problematic rise in gain of the parasitic bipolar transistors that initiate latchup. This and other problems are being investigated in research programmes and international conferences (eg the International Electron Devices Meeting held in San Francisco in December, 1982).

Much current research focuses on MOS technology but bipolar techniques and other approaches are also receiving attention. For example, Hitachi is aiming to develop faster, denser bipolar memories.

It has been suggested that by the early-1990s silicon chip technology will have reached its limits. Until that time, silicon-based component designs, originated either in university research laboratories or in the commercial environment, are likely to predominate. A key development in this context is the 'silicon foundry' which allows all designers to have access to circuit production facilities. Where formerly the high cost of in-house fabrication technology limited the scope for external designers, this situation has now changed. This is shown, for example, by the multiproject chip activity initiated at the California Institute of Technology. Electron beam lithography now allows several chip designs to be incorporated on the same mask and hence manufactured on the same wafer. In this way, the costs of a mask set and the processing of wafers can be shared between the designs, a development that is likely to encourage the bringing together of fabrication capacity and design initiatives. And again it can be emphasised that new problems arise with the design efforts to achieve ever-increasing levels of circuit integration. Professor Leo Rideout of IBM, considering chip design trends, has even suggested that alpha particles and cosmic rays could present problems in the design of 256K devices, interfering with the traffic on the very thin lines. Furthermore, the 256K chip might have to be cooled with liquid nitrogen because it would not operate satisfactorily at normal room temperature.

In 1982 the Japanese Ministry of International Trade and Industry (Tokyo) announced plans to spend around $215 million in the 1980s – in addition to other investment programmes of relevance to fifth generation – on semiconductor research. The project is aiming at three major developments: better crystal lattice structures, multiple-layer semiconductor structures, and devices capable of working under extreme environmental conditions. Efforts will also be made to investigate gallium arsenide and Josephson-junction technologies to attain the system-level performance of 100 million floating-point operations per second (flops) for a single-processor system and 10 billion flops in a multiple-processor configuration. The six participating companies are expected to spend about $200 million of their own funds on this research.

One aim in the semiconductor project is to raise carrier mobility by improving the lattice structures of gallium arsenide (GaAs). Use is being made of multilayer super-lattices in which layers of aluminium gallium arsenide are sandwiched between layers of GaAs. At the same time, efforts are being made to develop buried-electrode structures in silicon MOS devices to allow multiple control electrodes to be installed in the silicon. One possibility is the creation of vertical MOS transistors to replace the common lateral structures and so dramatically increase the circuit density.

These efforts will require major improvements in crystal-growth and layer-growth techniques, in super-lattice materials and structures, and in the material techniques available for creating buried-electrode structures. One significant contribution will be research into the building of three-dimensional integrated circuits. Efforts will be made to grow silicon layers on insulating materials and to develop multiple-layer interconnect technology that could support more than half-a-dozen layers. In this way it would be possible to include measuring, computational, memory and control sections without having to accept size trade-offs from one section to another. Semiconductor components will also be developed that are relatively immune to variations in temperature (operation to over 300° C), shock, vibration, and radiation.

The computers that will emerge towards the end of the decade will benefit from the various programmes of semiconductor research. System specifications being considered require a memory capacity of at least one billion bytes and a data transfer speed of not less than 1.5 billion bytes/second. It is expected that logic chips will carry at least 3000 gates, with chip fabrication explored for low-temperature GaAs, room-temperature GaAs, and super-cooled Josephson-junction technology. Fujitsu is expected to develop its HEMT (high-electron-mobility transistor) technology: since HEMT devices need be cooled to only −200° C, they are seen as strong contenders against Josephson devices (which require cooling to −272° C). HEMT technology, relying on characteristic features of GaAs, is likely to yield large-scale integrated circuits in the next few years. Such devices will have ultra-high-speed properties and low power dissipation. Nogami et al (1982), of Fujitsu, have commented that the 'super computer', based on HEMT-LSI, 'will soon be here'.

GaAs-based technology offers high-performance circuit elements, but at present there is a cost penalty which requires that GaAs devices be restricted to those applications that require their unique performance features. There is also the possibility of environmental pollution. Nogami et al (1982) have suggested, when GaAs and its related devices are brought into consumer products, the need to think about the recovery of used devices and regulations for use.

The November (1982) Gallium Arsenide Integrated Circuit Symposium, held in New Orleans, showed that researchers are near to effective production of medium-scale integration of GaAs. One suggestion is that cache memories for fast computers could be one of the first practical applications of GaAs technology: a 1K static random-access memory is being developed by the Musashino Electrical Communication Laboratory of the Nippon Telegraph and Telephone Public Corporation, and other firms are focusing on gate-array designs as well suited to the low-volume orders likely for actual GaAs products. Instrumentation applications are high priorities for GaAs devices. Engineers interested in testing the fastest silicon integrated circuits are considering the use of GaAs devices. And efforts are underway in France (by Gerard Nuzillat and his co-workers at the Central Research Laboratory of Thomson-CSF) to develop the building blocks that will lead to a 4-bit GaAs microprocessor.

In summary, there are two broad complementary trends in the development of integrated circuits:

— refinement and enhancement of traditional silicon-based technologies;

— development of Josephson-junction and gallium arsenide devices to provide high-speed memories and processors where appropriate (ie not to encroach on *all* silicon-dominated domains).

Microsystems

Microsystem developments are relevant to the emergence of

supercomputers and fifth-generation configurations. Some super-computer architectures rely on the simultaneous operation of many microsystems working in parallel. Furthermore, many of the man/machine interface facilities envisaged for fifth-generation computers will, ideally, exploit the processing capability of microsystems. Optimistically, expert systems are now being written for microcomputers. It would be a mistake to assume that fifth-generation computers will necessarily resemble fourth-generation mainframes, albeit with vastly increased processing power and many new facilities.

One key element in microsystem development is the provision of support chips with microprogrammable architectures to enable different processors to exploit the existing body of application software. At the same time, there is a steady move towards distributed architectures. Intel has launched what has been called a 'second-generation' 16-bit processor, the 80286, its pipelined architecture and unique memory management offering a six-fold improvement in performance over the 'first-generation' 8086 processor. In the 80286, programs are broken into logically-separate segments, each with a maximum size of 64K bytes.

Architectural flexibility is offered by the new NCR/32-chip set, externally microprogrammable and able, when supplied with the appropriate microcode, to execute object code drawn from the wide range of existing application software. NCR has estimated, for example, that a COBOL virtual machine for execution of COBOL virtual programs could be implemented in 25K bytes of microcode. Architectures such as NCR's are seen as a generalised solution to the problem of software compatibility.

An architecture from Texas Instruments can be dynamically configured to resemble arbitrary architectures. The design is based on a 16-bit processor (termed a 'microprogrammable slice'), a bus control unit (that gates data flow along a configurable set of paths), and a memory scheduling unit (that handles requests from processors coexisting on the bus). The aim is to place four microprogrammable slices on a single chip where they may link as needed to work in various ways.

Another architectural innovation, termed 'systolic array processing', was represented in a 1978 paper by Professor Kung and a graduate student, C. L. Leiserson (both at Carnegie Mellon University). Of this idea Kung has observed: 'I knew the concept was intuitively simple and intuitively regular, so it had to be good for computers'. The architecture relies on a highly-parallel and pipelined configuration and is of growing interest to designers of high-performance signal-processing systems. (The name 'systolic' derives from the similarity of how data is pumped through a network of processors to how the heart moves blood through the circulation vessels.) Systolic processors, matching separate processors with individual processing steps in algorithms, exhibit a regularly-repeated structure. This is useful for VLSI implementation. Systolic processing techniques are likely to be implemented for a wide variety of commercial applications requiring fast, repetitive, number-crunching operations.

New architectures are often of clear relevance to fifth-generation systems and to the emergence of 'supercomputer' configurations. Now J-11, a 'supermicroprocessor' implementation of the PDP-11/70 microcomputer, has been configured with more than 138,000 transistors on two complementary-MOS integrated circuits. The silicon-gate C-MOS technology has combined low power dissipation with fast gate speeds 'to produce a state-of-the-art supermicrocomputer with a 200-nanosecond cycle time' (Rubinfeld, 1982). Again we see developments in microsystems that could have direct relevance to fifth-generation computers: the emerging microsystems architectures could be exploited for dedicated tasks in, for example, man/machine interfaces or high-speed processing for AI purposes, computation and other tasks.

Artificial Intelligence

Artificial intelligence (AI) already has many aspects (and a prodigious literature). Not all the aspects are equally relevant to the development of fifth-generation computers. For example, inference-making is of obvious importance in this connection, with the ability to generate computerised haiku or Aesop-type fables of less significance. Game-playing (eg chess, bridge, backgammon, etc) may be regarded as of intermediate relevance to fifth-generation systems. It will not be essential to play draughts or chess with the next generation of computers, but developing the necessary heuristic techniques for game-playing will throw light on necessary fifth-generation operating strategies in conditions of uncertainty. (AI is considered in more detail in Chapter 3.)

Expert Systems

These are, in one clear sense, a manifestation of AI. Typically, such systems make inferences following interrogation of a 'knowledge base'. In addition, a degree of probability may be assigned to the conclusion that is drawn. Expert systems, structured around a body of (human) expert knowledge, are intended to assist human deliberations in such fields as medical diagnosis, chemical analysis and geological prospecting. Such systems predate the first fifth-generation declarations but are clearly relevant to the next generation of computers. It is expected that fifth-generation systems will, amongst many other tasks, be able to provide a conversational advisory facility when working with human beings. (Expert systems are considered in more detail in Chapter 4.)

Man/Machine Communication

We have seen that an express intention behind fifth-generation computers is that they be 'user friendly', a feature that is required if they are to be of most use to (often computer-naive) human beings. This means that, ideally, fifth-generation computers will be able to understand what is said to them, to read handwriting, and to understand other natural forms of human communication; to 'think about' the information so obtained; and to frame an appropriate response. These computers will, therefore, need to be skilled at such tasks as voice recognition, pattern recognition and speech synthesis. (These and other related aspects are considered in more detail in Chapter 5.)

FIFTH-GENERATION COMPUTER SYSTEMS

The fifth-generation computer project has been seen as an attempt to produce truly intelligent computers, systems that can be addressed in plain (natural) language and with which it is possible to converse. Such computers may be expected to have certain advantages over human beings, if only because of the ease with which vast amounts of information ('knowledge') can be stored and manipulated in artificial systems. Such impressive processing capability will be essential in many of the specific applications associated with fifth-generation systems. For example, one idea is a machine translation system able to handle multiple languages, with a total vocabulary of around 100,000 words. It is suggested that such a system would be 90 per cent accurate, with people handling the remaining 10 per cent. The cost of such a facility is to be held at 30 per cent (or an even lower percentage) of human translation. In this way, telephone exchanges would be able to translate almost instantaneously. By the end of the century, telephone users would be able to speak to each other in their native languages, automatic translation taking place en route. It is easy to see why Kazuhiro Fuchi, a leading Japanese computer scientist with the Agency of Industrial Science and Technology (AIST), MITI's research and development arm, declares that fifth-generation equipment 'will not be an extension of gradual improvements over current computers . . . The next stage will be a leap forward'.

In addition to automatic language translation, fifth-generation computers will be involved in such applications as:

— *document preparation,* using human speech as sole input;

— *professional consultation,* by first transferring, say, human medical expertise to the machine and then requesting a diagnosis;

— *decision-taking,* facilitated by high-speed inference mechanisms. Information would be manipulated logically and conclusions drawn.

Broadly viewed, the basic fifth-generation computer is seen as having three main functions: storing information, solving problems and interfacing with human beings. Each of these functions will be supported by specialised hardware and software systems (shown in Figure 1.1). Again it can be emphasised that even if the full fifth-generation goals are not reached (by the first-prototype date of 1991), there are likely to be many milestone innovations achieved on the way. In 1979 the Japanese Government began an investigation into the fifth generation of computers, and an international conference was held in October 1981, in Tokyo. A central aim was to encourage Western collaboration and to discuss the

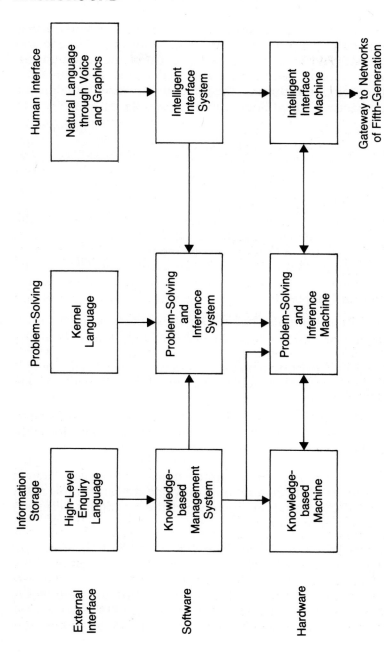

Figure 1.1 Main Elements in Fifth-Generation Computers

ideas behind the proposed development project. The Japanese fifth-generation committee, set up by the Ministry of Trade and Industry (MITI), consists of more than 250 of the leading technologists in Japan. The committee has declared that the fifth-generation computer, through the use of its advanced capabilities, should 'advance society along a more desirable path'.

It has been suggested that a high level of Western collaboration will be crucial to the successful development of fifth-generation computers (for instance, Japanese funding over the years 1982-1984 for fifth generation is intended to be about $450 million – which amounts to about one third of IBM's annual research and development budget). Dr Kazuhiro Fuchi has even declared: 'It would be fatal for us if Western experts told us that the project was not aimed in the right direction'. It is clear that there is massive scope for Western involvement in fifth-generation development, and that the Japanese are encouraging such participation. (Something of the response to fifth-generation plans is considered in Chapter 6.)

One significant impulse behind Japanese plans is the need for Japan – less than one per cent self-sufficient in oil and only 15 per cent self-sufficient in energy overall – to survive as a viable economic unit. Efforts to develop programming to produce output in the Japanese language led to the view that input and output problems could only be solved in conjunction with a new approach to the architecture of the central processor. It was clear that radical research was necessary for the development of new computer systems that would both serve the Japanese economy and generate trading profits to enable Japan to pay for its imported oil, food and raw materials. The importance attached in Japan to investment in high technology – fifth generation is only one concern among many – derives directly from how Japan views the conditions necessary for its survival as a country.

The Japanese plans and motivation are of obvious relevance to Western economies. Despite the origins of the fifth-generation programme, the emerging systems will be culture-free: they will bear equally on social and economic problems throughout the developed world. It has been emphasised that many of the elements in fifth-generation systems have been under development in many countries for many years. There is an important sense in which the fifth-generation programme is already an international enterprise.

SUMMARY

This chapter has charted the history of computers to highlight the milestones on the road to fifth-generation systems. And in this context, the character of the earlier computer generations has been profiled. An effort has also been made to indicate the relevance of some current trends – in supercomputer research, integrated circuits, microsystems, artificial intelligence, etc – to the fifth-generation programmes of research and development. Emphasis has been given to the necessary convergence of these trends for the successful realisation of fifth-generation computers.

A few indications have been included of the characteristics of fifth-generation systems. In this background chapter, these features have been outlined to convey the 'flavour' of the systems that will emerge over the next decade (more details are given in Chapter 2). The role of Japan in fifth generation has been sketched, though the international character of current computer trends and developments has also been emphasised.

2 Fifth-Generation Features and Research

INTRODUCTION

Definitions of fifth-generation features have derived from the tasks that the new computers will be intended to perform. These features have not yet been realised; fifth-generation computers do not yet exist. The broad scheme, framed in Japan, has been to characterise the required systems and then to organise the spectrum of research programmes whereby such systems will be achieved. This chapter aims to profile the main features of fifth-generation computers and to indicate the associated research and development (R and D) projects.

The anticipated leap forward to fifth-generation computers has been characterised in many ways. Marsh (1982), for example, has noted likely trends in three broad areas: in very large-scale integration (VLSI), allowing circuits to be more densely packed; in methods of processing data, so that these will come to resemble human thought patterns; and in redesigning computer memories so these will more effectively serve the intended tasks. It is easy to think of other areas that will be crucial: for example, extensive research is being carried out in such fields as systems architecture, computer languages, artificial intelligence and man/machine interfaces (these aspects are considered in the present chapter and in later ones). The radical nature of the fifth-generation concept means that effective 'rethinks' are necessary in all the areas of traditional computer system design.

Mideo Aiso, leading the team charged with developing fifth-generation architectures, has declared the need for functions capable of organising appropriate structures adaptable to many different applications. This requires a flexible architecture rather than a combination of uniformly-structured memory devices and von Neumann arithmetic and control units, which traditionally leave complex functions to programs. The need for a highly intelligent man/machine interface (for natural languages such as Japanese and English) is emphasised, and the machine will also have to provide 'human substitute functions to support judgement and research'. Aiso has suggested that such a machine will need to run at 100 million to 1000 million logical inferences/second, with one logical inference probably needing 100 conventional machine instructions. One idea is that the final machine will achieve the necessary high speed of operation by means of array processing using as many as 1000 processors.

The structure of the fifth-generation machine has been described by Kazuhiro Fuchi as having seven levels. The uppermost levels, carrying the application stages and the natural man/machine interfaces, will be implemented in a knowledge information processing system on a virtual machine. The virtual machine first level will be able to call down one level to what are, in effect, three further virtual machines: a virtual processor, a virtual database and a virtual network machine. A string of special function processors will comprise a second level of virtualisation which will include an array processor, a global communications processor, a local communications processor, a database machine, an operating system processor, etc. It is suggested that the various layers will be implemented on functionally distributed real machines based on VLSI circuits.

The knowledge information processing system, based on problem-solving and inference mechanisms, will link the machine functions to the man/machine natural language interface. This processing system will be the heart of the fifth-generation machine. The 'kernel' language will be based on PROLOG which, using the *Horn* syllogism in format logic, is an inferential logic language. The current programme allows ten years for the development of an effective kernel language, with PROLOG being developed in the early years by the addition of meta structures, a relational database interface and various modularisation mechanisms. The relational database machine, to be based on the conventional von Neumann architecture, will be at the heart of the knowledge-base machine. It is expected that the other machines will exploit various data flow, pipelining and highly-parallel architectures (see Architectures, below).

The complexity of the explicit fifth-generation research programme – which comprises many individual projects for architecture, hardware, software, etc – suggests that all the required fifth-generation features may not be realised with the same degree of success. In such circumstances, the definition of fifth-generation computers will evolve over the period of the programme. The first efforts to frame such a definition were made in 1979.

THE CONCEPT OF FIFTH GENERATION

It is possible to trace implicit fifth-generation concepts throughout the 1970s. For many years, research has been conducted on such topics as expert systems, intelligent interfaces and unconventional computer architectures. It was in 1979, however, with the Japanese launch of a two-year preliminary investigation into the next generation of computers, that the fifth-generation concept became explicit. A 1980 report from the Japan Information Processing Centre (JIPDEC) outlines the 'image of the fifth-generation computer'. Here it is predicted that fifth-generation computers will have a number of aspects, 'as a result of the coordination of . . . social needs . . . with seeds based on inevitable technological progress'. Four aspects are listed:

— there will be a considerable diversity of computer functions, types and levels, from machines for very high-speed processing to processors with specialised functions and applications, personal computers and the built-in computers;

— there will be a decline in the former trend to very general-purpose orientation, with an increase in specialisation;

— there will be an increase in the emphasis placed on non-von-Neumann architectures;

— the importance of new micro-architectures will increase; there will be considerable use of systems formed by combining a number of processors and hardware, software and

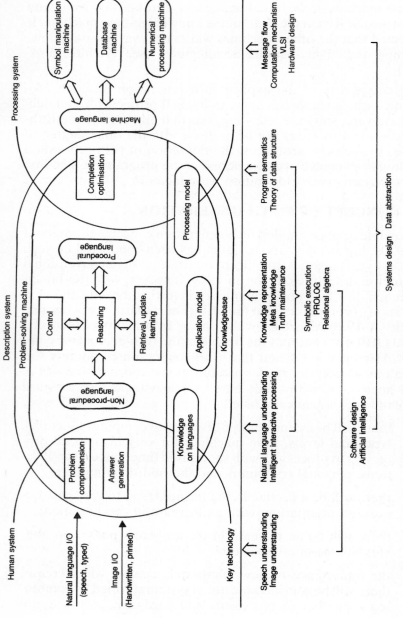

Figure 2.1 Knowledge Information Processing System and Technology for its Realisation
(Source: *JIPDEC Report on Fifth-Generation Computers*, summer 1980)

firmware module elements; and the importance of system architecture will grow.

From these various aspects it is concluded that a fifth-generation computer would be based on non-von-Neumann architectures and would be able to provide knowledge information processing. The computer would be, in effect, a knowledge information processing (KIP) system and would comprise: high-level man/machine interfacing and the ability to solve problems.

The interfacing requires that all forms of input – including natural language, patterns, images, handwritten characters, speech, etc – should be input conversationally. The system should be able to extract meaning from the information and should have a genuine intelligent dialogue capability: the computer should be able to answer questions, make suggestions, prompt the human user, give summarised answers, etc. It is obvious that problem-solving functions are essential for this purpose, and that the problem in question should be equally well understood by both man and machine: a common basis of understanding is seen as the 'foundation of harmony between man and machine'.

The requirement for mutual understanding implies that the machine will need to be capable of adjusting its understanding in line with that of a human being. A further important function will be that of acquiring new knowledge related to the field of a problem. One consideration concerns unity – 'the incorporation of knowledge which does not conflict with, or contradict, the system's existing knowledge'; while another concerns inductive reasoning, – the ability to draw conclusions from a collection of data. These aspects relate to the problem of learning (see Chapter 3). Figure 2.1 shows the structure of such a system for providing these functions.

It is also recognised that a high level of non-numerical (symbol) processing will be required for various functions, and that a 'non-deterministic algorithm' will be central to such tasks as learning and reasoning. Current hardware and software research is focusing on these requirements. For example, attention is being given to systematic programming based on data abstraction, and to a rule-based technique for program changing. A variety of provisions will be required for such tasks as pattern recognition and non-

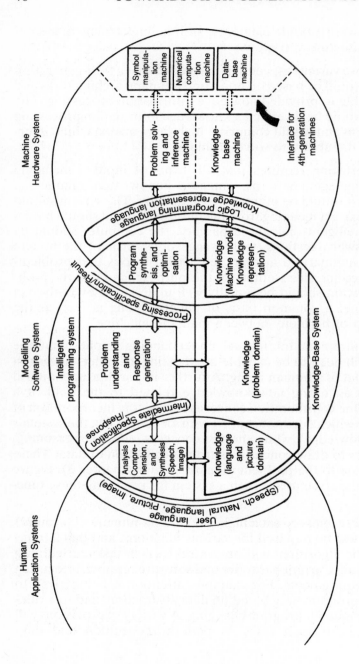

Figure 2.2 Conceptual View of Fifth-Generation Computers

(Source: *Proceedings of International Conference on Fifth-Generation Computer Systems*, 19-22 October, 1981, JIPDEC)

deterministic processing, the aim being the development of a reasoning (inference) machine. And reasoning capability will also be provided by the development of a relational algebra machine that would perform retrieval functions on the relational database. Relational algebraic calculations would be performed for data retrieval purposes.

There is little in the 1979 view of fifth-generation computers that does not obtain today, though some of the emphases may have shifted. The main functions of fifth-generation machines have been broadly classified under three headings:

— problem-solving and inference-making;

— knowledge-base management;

— intelligent interfaces.

Figure 2.2 illustrates the conceptual image of how hardware and software will cooperate to realise the required functions. The modelling software system is represented as one of the main programme objectives for software development, the machine hardware system an ultimate target for hardware development. The upper half of the modelling system circle signifies the problem-solving and inference functions, the lower half the knowledge-base management facility. The intelligent interface function – where the software system circle overlaps the human application systems circle – relies on the two former groups of functions. The diagram emphasises how computer design is shifting towards the human system: the logic level of the hardware system will be dramatically enhanced and the sophisticated modelling system will be positioned between the hardware and the human operators.

One design aim will be to provide a number of problem-solving systems cooperating with each other. A problem-solving system may use large-scale external databases that will function as libraries. The knowledge-base management system (having inference functions analogous to the library user) will cooperate with the databases (analogous to the libraries) in solving problems.

In, for example, a medical diagnosis system a diagnosis will be made in the same way as a physician and a surgeon might work together to achieve a diagnosis. Such a system would require a

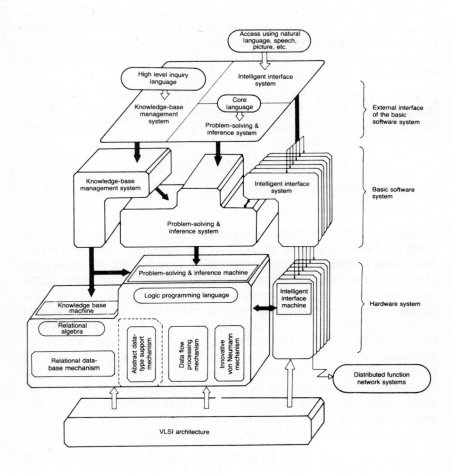

Figure 2.3   Conceptual Structure for Fifth-Generation Computers

(Source: *Proceedings of International Conference on Fifth-Generation Computer Systems,* 19-22 October, 1981, JIPDEC)

meta-inference facility to perform inferences on the lower-level inferences of individual problem-solving systems and also on the knowledge contained in the individual systems. The meta-inference system should be capable of deduction, induction, analogical inference and other tacit inferences that formerly have only characterised human problem-solvers. The aim is that these functions will be realised as software in the kernel language. There will be provision for trial-and-error (heuristic) processes in circumstances where inferences cannot be made on a logically-exhaustive basis.

The high level of performance that will be needed to support the symbol processing that is the key to inference will be achieved, as we have seen, by high-speed parallel architectures. These will be integrated with developed software to form effective problem-solving configurations. The systems will also have capacity for semi-automated knowledge acquisition, which means that they will not always have to be spoon-fed their information by human beings: the systems will have a certain level of learning capability, possibly linked to visual and other sensors to detect changes in the external environment.

The various software and hardware systems developed to realise the three broad functions listed above will be coupled to provide a general-purpose machine with the conceptual structure shown in Figure 2.3 (it is useful to compare this structure with the conceptual view shown in Figure 2.2). The general-purpose machine will be adaptable to accommodate the various performance features required by specific functions.

It is envisaged that fifth-generation machines will be interconnected in networks to form distributed processing systems. Implementation in VLSI will be essential, and a variety of application languages suited to various levels of fifth-generation computer users will be developed. Table 2 gives examples of some of the basic applications systems that are envisaged (glancing at these it is obvious that relevant R and D has been going on for many years).

One intention is to develop a sequential inference machine to support an early version of the kernel language, in order to aid software research and development. The aim will be high-performance personal systems equipped with user-friendly man/

machine interfaces, such systems having high-precision graphic displays, speech, Japanese text input and output, and other features. (The various R and D projects are considered below.)

Before examining the various fifth-generation features – integrated circuits, architectures, software, knowledge processing, etc – in more detail, it is worth emphasising that fifth-generation computers, as described by the Japanese, have been envisaged as emerging in a social context as a means of achieving a number of identifiable social objectives.

SOCIAL NEEDS AND IMPACT

In the keynote speech to the International Conference on Fifth-Generation Computer Systems (19-22 October 1981, Tokyo), Mote-oka et al begin by indicating what they see as the social requirements expected of computers in the 1990s. At that time, fifth-generation computers will be in wide use, with information processing systems regarded as central tools in all areas of social activity (economics, industry, art, science, administration, international relations, etc). Specific roles are identified. Information processing systems will be expected:

— *to increase productivity in low-productivity areas*. It is noted that computers have already improved product quality and productivity in manufacturing but that there has been little change in such areas as agriculture, fishing, good distribution and the public services. This situation has led to serious social imbalances;

— *to meet international competition and contribute towards international cooperation*. Japan is short on natural resources, far from self-sufficient in food and with her ability to supply her own energy needs the lowest among the developed countries. A highly-educated, diligent and top-quality labour force is seen as a precious asset. In these circumstances, energy itself should be cultivated as an important new resource;

— *to assist in saving energy and resources*. It is essential to use the world's finite resources effectively. Computers will be used to improve energy conversion efficiency and to develop new sources of energy. A knowledge-intensive

Machine translation system

— Translations among multiple languages

— Vocabulary size: 100,000 words

— Machine to guarantee a 90% accuracy, with the remaining 10% to be processed through intervention by man

— System to be an integrated system where computers participate in the individual stages ranging from text editing to printing of translations

— Total costs involved to remain at 30% or lower than those of translation by man

Consultation systems

— Specimen applications

   — Medical diagnosis

   — Natural language comprehension

   — Mechanical equipment CAD (computer-aided design)

   — Computer user consultation

   — Computer systems diagnosis

— Number of objects: 5000 or more

— Inference rules: 10,000 or more

— Semi-automated knowledge acquisition

— Interfaces with system: Natural languages and speech

— Vocabulary size: 5000 words or more

Table 2   Targets for Basic Application Systems (see also Table 4)
(Source: *Outline of Research and Development Plans for Fifth-Generation Computer Systems,* May 1982, ICOT, JIPDEC)

type information industry is seen as 'typically non-energy consuming';

— *to cope with an aged society*. With Japanese society ageing 'at an unprecedented rate' – people 65 years of age or older will make up 12 per cent of the Japanese population in 1990 – increases in medical and welfare costs, together with the relative reduction in the labour force, could lead to large social problems. Computers may be expected to help by streamlining the medical and related information systems, health management systems, education systems for the aged, etc.

These requirements are expanded in the same keynote speech. For example, the need for a competitive posture should not preclude cooperation in such subjects as: the building and maintenance of certain databases, smoothing international exchanges by means of translating and interpreting systems; using intelligent robots to improve productivity; and accelerating research and development by means of intelligent computer-aided design (CAD) systems.

It is recognised that, as society becomes increasingly information-centred, computers and society will relate to each other 'in more complicated and diversified ways'. The information industry should be developed in such a way that governments are not encouraged to control their people in a repressive fashion and also so that computers are not allowed to 'turn against mankind'. The aim should be that computers are developed 'with a view to making them both usable and likeable'.

From the beginning, the Japanese Fifth-Generation Computer Committee tried to foresee the impact that the new systems would have on society, and for this purpose established the Subcommittee for Research into Social Environmental Conditions. Possible broad impacts of fifth-generation computers can be identified (partly summarising the points above):

— the elimination of social distortions deriving from productivity differences in different fields;

— the expansion of human intelligence by means of machines;

— the management of the vast amount of information generated by the information technologies.

In addition to being applied to specialist tasks, fifth-generation
intelligence will allow the new systems to adapt to human requirements. For instance, the computer will judge how information is to
be sifted, organised and presented to be of most value to the
human user. And, progressively, the gap between individuals and
machines will be bridged: people without programming ability or
specialist knowledge of computers will be able to converse with the
machines.

The Japanese social context has influenced how people see the
likely contribution of fifth-generation computers. Japanese man-

Problems (681 factories)	Present	1985	1990
Worker ageing	51.2	53.6	61.6
Shortage of skilled workers	38.2	37.0	28.8
Higher wages	35.1	39.4	45.5
Shortage of unskilled workers	12.8	15.4	16.3
Shortage of workers for dangerous or poor working conditions	12.5	12.2	8.4
Decline in morale	10.4	8.5	6.0
Other	5.6	3.1	2.2
None	6.9	5.7	2.6

**Table 3   Percentage of Japanese Managers who Regard
Particular Issues as Problems**
(Source: *Nikkei Mechanical,* 1981)

agers, for example, have been asked to rate various issues as problems for the present and for the future (see Table 3). Without similar polls in other developed economies we cannot assume that emphases and perceptions in Europe and America would necessarily accord with those in Japan. However, such social circumstances as a growing aged population and a shortage of skilled workers are evident factors in many industrial societies.

The expected contribution of fifth-generation computers in this context is two-fold. The new machines will focus on tasks that are too difficult, too uneconomic or too uncomfortable for human beings to undertake; and computers will improve the efficiency of the health management systems and the related services.

INTEGRATED CIRCUITS AND CAD

We have seen (Chapter 1) that research into integrated circuits is essential to the successful realisation of fifth-generation systems. This research is currently investigating a wide range of fabrication methods, materials and technologies (eg Josephson junctions and such compounds as gallium arsenide and indium phosphate). In late-1982 the Japanese semiconductor manufacturer Toshiba announced a prototype of a commercially-viable gallium arsenide chip, a 500-gate array featuring an 80-picosecond delay between gates. This device is claimed to be five times faster than conventional semiconductors. The higher electron mobility of gallium arsenide is likely to be one of many characteristics that will serve the high-speed requirements of fifth-generation systems. Research into such topics is vital to the overall success of the development programme. In particular, emphasis is being given to the importance of widely-applied VLSI technology relying on enhanced silicon-based techniques. To be effectively achieved this requires:

— computational structures and algorithms suited to the two-dimensional nature of VLSI;

— sophisticated CAD systems to handle VLSI design complexity;

— quick-turnaround fabrication facilities (ie the 'silicon foundries' described in Chapter 1).

One research aim is to develop silicon-based VLSI devices carrying more than 10 million transistors: two major research projects are focusing on the production of VLSI chips (described by Sakamura et al, paper to Conference on Fifth Generation Computer Systems, 1981). One project is devoted to VLSI algorithms, investigating what functions should be implemented on VLSI chips and how this can be achieved. The other project focuses on VLSI CAD systems, ie on the support system for the design and fabrication of VLSI circuits.

CAD systems for VLSI circuits are highly sophisticated, requiring considerable computer power and beyond the scope of many current computers. At the same time, VLSI CAD facilities are seen as priorities for the successful development of fifth-generation systems, and such CAD provisions will be required to run on the new computers when they emerge towards the end of the decade. For these reasons, efforts are being made to develop a flexible system architecture, termed SYSTEM 5G, that will be able to adapt to the evolving hardware needs. This programme is intended to comprise three main development areas:

— construction of VLSI CAD systems;

— development of SYSTEM 5G on which the CAD systems will run;

— development of the 5G personal computer to interface users with SYSTEM 5G.

The CAD systems, intended to design VLSI chips with more than one million transistors, will be able to describe the specifications for electronic circuits, logic circuits, fabrication processes, layout routeing, wiring, timing, testing procedures, etc. In addition, circuit simulation and generation of layout patterns for the mask should be within the scope of the CAD facilities. Pattern checks will be performed on the mask layouts generated, and verified patterns will be automatically fed into the mask generator. Test patterns will also be fed into the VLSI testing equipment.

The available CAD systems in Japan and elsewhere do not satisfy the specified requirements. Current systems cannot provide the various specifications from the architectural level to the mask layout generation level. Furthermore, existing systems are not easy to operate and users require extensive training. The ultimate aim with SYSTEM 5G is for users to sit in front of personal logic programming stations used as terminals to access 'super inference machines'. The development of a suitable network architecture will allow various services to be offered on a distributed basis. It is emphasised that conventional network architectures – such as SNA developed for von Neumann machines – are unlikely to be suitable for fifth-generation computer systems. Research is therefore required on the personal logic programming station, the super inference machine and the network architecture.

The *personal logic programming station* is seen as essentially a personal inference machine, with LISP and PROLOG being available as basic languages. This station will serve as the standard terminal in SYSTEM 5G. Ease-of-use will require that the station be equipped with voice, graphics and digitised images. It is anticipated that several hundred VLSI-based stations will be used by researchers.

The *super inference* machine will incorporate lower-level inference systems, relational database machines and network controllers, all connected on a 1G byte/second high-speed local network. It is estimated that these various elements will be state-of-the-art products by the end of the decade. The high-speed inference machine will have a 1000G byte database, and will be structured around various novel architectures.

The 5G *network architecture* will include local networks of personal logic programming stations, global networks maintained by NTT, etc, and the high-speed SYSTEM 5G local networks. It is anticipated that, in addition to the super inference machine and the stations, a range of other devices (eg telephones, facsimiles, sensors, optical character readers, intelligent copiers, etc) will be connected in the 5G network. This will facilitate communication by means of voice, graphics and digitised images.

The various research activities will be designed to satisfy the above requirements. For instance, four steps have been identified (in connection with the VLSI CAD system) for designing VLSI chips:

— specification of VLSI functions or the description of the architecture;

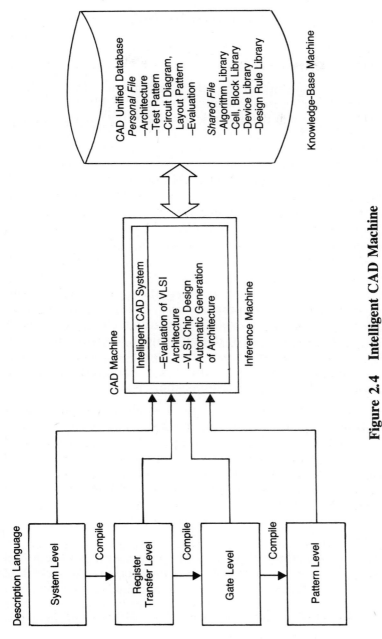

Figure 2.4   Intelligent CAD Machine

(Source: *Proceedings of International Conference on Fifth-Generation Computer Systems,* 19-22 October, 1981, JIPDEC)

— functional, logical and electronic design;

— layout pattern generation;

— test pattern generation.

The close relationship between these various steps implies that a hierarchical design approach is likely to be useful. For this purpose a unified description and automatic data handling via a database is required. A CAD system of this sort may be regarded as an application of the knowledge information processing technique. Sakamura et al (1981) explore in detail the research project requirements for developing SYSTEM 5G, considering software, architecture and other features. An overview of the intelligent CAD machine is shown in Figure 2.4.

What we are seeing is the increasing use of VLSI-based systems to design more complex (and more intelligent) VLSI systems. Some of these systems need to be developed to aid the design activities that are essential to the realisation of the overall fifth-generation programme: once developed, the systems become subject to further evolutionary pressures. SYSTEM 5G, for instance, is represented as having an evolutionary architecture. At the start it will support the whole VLSI design project, to grow later into a knowledge information network after about ten years' development. One conceptual layout for the super inference machine, the intelligent heart of fifth-generation systems, is shown in Figure 2.5.

It is evident that computers will increasingly participate in their own evolution. The high-performance designs necessary for fifth-generation systems (whether configured in Josephson-junction circuits, high-speed GaAs or silicon-based VLSI circuits) will increasingly rely upon computer intelligence for their realisation. Integrated circuits, in most of their features, will more and more become the brain children of other integrated circuits.

MEMORIES

One broad goal in the fifth-generation programme is to redesign computer memories, where data and instructions are held and which act as an effective link between a machine's processing unit and the outside world. In addition to generating more suitable software (eg in PROLOG and LISP, see Software and Languages

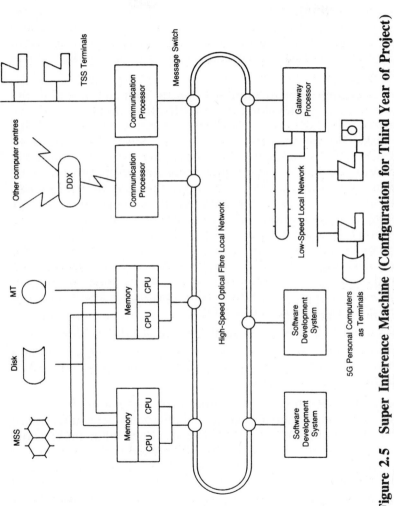

Figure 2.5 Super Inference Machine (Configuration for Third Year of Project)
(Source: *Proceedings of International Conference on Fifth-Generation Computer Systems,*
19-22 October, 1981, JIPDEC)

below) to make it easier to communicate with intelligent systems, it is useful to put into computer memories appropriate information that people carry as a matter of course (see Chapter 4). In the field of research known as *knowledge engineering* the aim is to pour into the computer memory a vast body of useful information, and also to structure the details so that the computer can relate different pieces of information to each other, much in the way that human beings do.

The new approach to memory density and organisation will depend upon the development of effective memory systems, whether using solid-state technology or other approaches. Today hard disks, floppy disks and tape are the lowest-cost and best-performing means for the various types of mass storage required in computer systems. But longitudinal recording, using tiny magnetic domains on the surface, is limited by physical constraints. *Vertical,* or *perpendicular, magnetic* recording and *magneto-optical laser* recording are possible ways of increasing the bit densities of erasable storage – to as much as fifty times more than today's gamma ferrous oxide disks and tape drives. Most work on vertical recording – which requires a medium in which small regions that stand up vertically through the medium thickness can be magnetised – has been done in Japan, though important research is also being conducted in France, Italy and the US.

(The 'father of vertical recording' is generally reckoned to be Professor Shun-ichi Iwasaki of Tohoku University in Sendai.) Various disks using vertical recording are being developed in Japan, the US and Europe.

The first device for storing digital data on non-erasable laser optical disks for archival storage applications was introduced towards the end of 1982. Progress has also been made on erasable magneto-optic laser disks which could be used for data or video: here a thermomagnetic effect is used for writing and the Kerr rotation effect is used for reading. Xerox scientists have produced a four-layer amorphous-thin-film disk, that may prove suitable for magneto-optic data storage; and NHK in Japan have announced a prototype erasable video disk using magneto-optic laser recording on a double-layer film.

In mid-1982, NEC announced it intended to double production

of its 64K bit dynamic random access memory – to achieve output of 2.5 million units/month by April 1983. Hitachi also set about producing 2.2 million 64K bit rams/month by 1983, a remarkable production increase for one of the most sophisticated memory chips on the market. And Hitachi has also developed the 256K bit chip ahead of Western (and other Japanese) competitors. The production process for the 256K bit ram uses a Reduction Projection Aligner, a unique Hitachi innovation. This technique allows conduction tracks half-a-micron wide to achieve centre-to-centre spacing of only 1.2 microns, about a quarter of the distance achieved in current 64K bit rams. The approach has been dubbed 'ultra large-scale integration'.

The data storage scene is seeing rapid development, with dramatic enhancement of traditional technologies and the progressive establishment of new methods. Memory, with vast storage capability and rapid access, is vital to artificial intelligence (see Chapter 3) and therefore to expert systems and fifth-generation computers. The effective development of semiconductor and other storage technologies will be crucial to the realisation of the broad fifth-generation programme.

ARCHITECTURES

General

The principles of computer system design remained largely static from the earliest electronic computers to the 1970s. The design approach was almost invariably based on the so-called von Neumann architecture, that of the sequential control-flow computer. This type of computer has traditionally contained:

— a single computing element that incorporates a processor, communications and memory;

— a linear organisation of fixed-sized memory cells;

— a one-level address space of memory cells;

— a low-level machine language (instructions performing simple operations on simple operands);

— a sequential centralised control of computation;

— a primitive input/output capability.

This type of computer architecture was originally designed for scientific and other forms of calculation, and has been since developed wherever the high-speed processing of numerical calculations has been required. One consequence of this approach was that dependence on software increased: the relatively simple architecture could only be induced to perform complex processes by means of increasingly sophisticated, and costly, software. It is suggested that this situation has contributed to what has been seen as a 'software crisis'. The Japanese, for example, have argued that:

—   today's traditionally-configured computer architectures are not equipped with the necessary functions, including input/output, to process non-numerical data such as sentences, symbols, speech, graphics and images. Such functions are necessary if computers are to become truly user-friendly;

—   conventional computers seem unable to cope efficiently with the performance demands of applications such as artificial intelligence, and AI is recognised as an increasingly important element in new computer systems;

—   efforts to improve the system design of computers to increase performance have achieved little success;

—   decentralised computing has been found to be expensive and difficult to implement, due mainly to the lack of a system architecture to which all the component computers conform;

—   it has been unclear how to exploit VLSI technology in multimicrocomputer design.

In these circumstances, one central approach is to develop new non-von-Neumann architectures, to retain traditional systems configurations where appropriate but to supplement these with new architectures designed for specific high-speed applications.

New Architectures

In the traditional operation of a sequential von Neumann machine, the control unit sends one instruction at a time to the arithmetic segment, which then performs one operation at a time on single pieces of data extracted for the occasion from the memory. One important idea in the new architectures is that computers would handle large amounts of data in parallel at the same time. Traditional computers have some difficulty in, for example, working out the meaning of a photograph or controlling a robot intended to manipulate small mechanical objects. Parallel processing, essential for such tasks, has already been attempted in various ways: for example, ICL's distributed array processor and the CLIP-4 machine developed at London's University College. Further progress in the parallel handling of instructions is essential if fifth-generation computers are to become a reality.

We may expect to see the emergence of computer designs in which multiple processors can work on parts of problems at the same time. There are already many signs that this trend is underway. For instance, the first of Denelcor Inc's HEP (heterogeneous-element processor) systems, which bring together multiple-instruction processing with multiple data streams, were delivered in 1982. In this configuration, up to sixteen parallel processors, each capable of running seven major tasks simultaneously by means of parallel function units, can be linked together to process at the rate of 160 million instructions per second. Many new computer systems announced in 1982 and early-1983 have some element of parallelism, and this trend may be expected to continue. Future systems may feature hundreds, or even thousands, of processors working simultaneously in single computer systems.

Parallel multiprocessor systems will have good fault-tolerance characteristics, crucial if computers are to be allowed to carry out important tasks in real time. Already, a number of fault-tolerant units are available (eg the NonStop system from Tandem Computers Inc) and more are expected (from new firms and from established companies such as IBM, ICL and DEC).

Many of the proposals on new architectures derive specifically from the fifth-generation programme. These proposals include versions of the parallel processing already mentioned. It is worth highlighting:

— *data flow architectures*. Von Neumann architectures typically exhibit *control flow* characteristics: processing is directed by the program instructions. By contrast, data flow architectures are driven by the flow of data from a *producer* to a *consumer* instruction, carried by a *data token*. When the required data inputs are available, a suitable action is initiated. Data flow architectures are seen as highly suitable for parallel processing and for the processing of knowledge bases (both key fifth-generation objectives);

— *distributed function architectures*. Here architectures are designed with modular facilities which allow specialised machines to carry out specific functions. Such systems are reliable and highly available, and can adapt to technological developments which affect particular functions. Typical functions are network control, database management, man/machine communications, high-speed computation, logical programming, and various types of parallel processing (including the use of data flow architectures).

The development of data-driven data-flow computers is expected to influence the nature of programming. There will be less emphasis on the traditional procedural languages, and new software developments will gradually affect programming philosophies on all types of computers (see Software and Languages, below). Two teams at the Massachusetts Institute of Technology (MIT) are exploring the architectural and software implications of the data-flow approach to system configuration.

Both the proposed machines employ a ring-networked multiprocessor architecture: in one machine the operands are queued between nodes in the network; and in the other the operands are allowed to flow freely, each carrying a tag token to indicate at which node it should be dealt with. Nodes in the tag token machine are each associated with a processing element, storing and executing an *interpreter* program. The interpreter identifies the paths between the data-flow machine nodes that operands must follow for a program to be executed; and can indicate several inter-loop procedure calls without programmer intervention. Jones (1982) describes aspects of the MIT research. One aim is to develop a data-flow supercomputer offering the performance of existing von Neumann-type supercomputers but comprising more than 6000 low-cost integrated circuits fabricated in N-channel MOS or complementary MOS (C-MOS) technology.

The search for new computer architectures began before the first fifth-generation pronouncements in the late-1970s, but the pronouncements gave new emphasis to the need to escape from the von Neumann straitjacket. Now it is commonplace to see new architectural ideas discussed in the literature: for instance, Sowa and Murata (1982) describe a data flow computer with program and token memories; and Mercer and Vincent (1982) consider a novel function-to-function architecture for building programmable electronic systems (for applications in robotics and other fields). It is obvious that there is a new flexibility in the approach to designing systems architectures, and that the fifth-generation programme is a key factor in this development. (Some of the important fifth-generation research papers, from the 1981 conference, are listed in the Bibliography.)

Hidehiko Tanaka et al (1981) describe the preliminary research programme intended to focus on data flow machines as part of the fifth-generation project. Initial work was concerned with such aspects as evaluating existing data flow machines and database machines, identifying appropriate research topics, and investigating performance, software, architectures and other system features. Preliminary study items for data flow machines were grouped under the heads:

— *hardware-related items*. Here attention is to be given to the system configuration ('general structure'), the control mechanism (eg exploring data-driven and demand-driven possibilities), basic operations (ie exploration of the machine language of the data flow machine), input/output mechanisms, and the implementation technology;

— *software-related items*. It is necessary to develop data-flow-oriented high-level languages, to design suitable operating systems, to investigate problems regarding activity allocation, and to develop a suitable parallel algorithm (it is assumed that inference applications, a key requirement in fifth-generation systems, will require a high-level of parallelism);

— *system development items*. To identify the design parameters and to evaluate system performance, it is necessary to describe the system formally and to simulate particular features. It is necessary, therefore, to develop languages suitable for asynchronous parallel operations. Debugging aids, maintenance facilities, input/output interfaces and portable software will also be required.

These various items are to be researched under the terms of a three-stage scheme (Tanaka et al, 1981). A requirement specification for the Stage-1 data flow machine is provided, and information follows on the selected study items (eg specification of functions, processing algorithm, hardware architecture, large-capacity data-handling mechanisms, auxiliary functions, the distributed database facility, implementation technology, etc). These topics and concepts essentially outline initial thoughts on how data flow architectures and related areas are to be researched over a ten-year programme.

SOFTWARE AND LANGUAGES

General

The performance requirements of fifth-generation computers will require the development of new computer languages, new operating systems, new applications software, etc. Some of these requirements were highlighted at the Sixth International Conference of Software Engineering (Tokyo, 1982), attended by representatives from seventeen different countries (Japan had about 1000 participants, followed by the US and Canada with 100 combined, and Europe with about half that number).

During the conference, ICOT (funded by Japan's Ministry for International Trade and Industry, MITI, to develop fifth-generation systems) outlined the ten-year fifth-generation programme. The three phases of the programme are shown in Figure 2.6.

The basic software system for fifth-generation computers directly reflects the structure of the intended application systems and comprises the intelligent interface, problem-solving and inference, and the knowledge-base management systems. The software will include a group of systems that, in designing and producing optimum information-processing systems for various applications, will 'know' what is to be produced, details of produc-

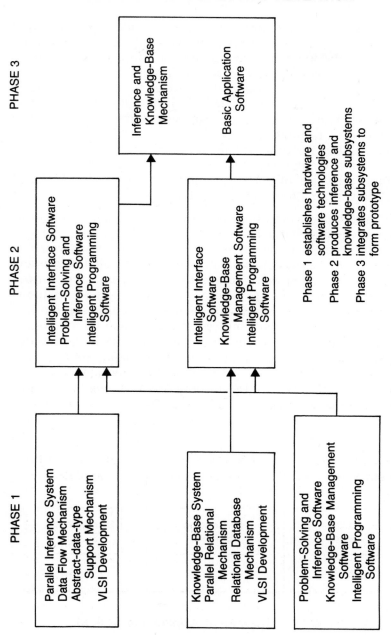

Figure 2.6 Three Phases of Fifth-Generation Computer Project

tion processes, etc. And the software will include subsystems that lead from a written specification to an eventual product, that verify correctness, and that simulate operations. Three support systems will also be included, ie an intelligent programming system for handling programs, a knowledge-base design system for handling a knowledge base, and an intelligent VLSI design system for VLSI chips and computer architectures. Sophisticated functions will also be provided to facilitate use of the system itself, and these will include facilities for transferring stored programs and databases from existing commercial machines to a target machine, for explaining the usage of functions, and for intelligent trouble diagnosis, recovery, maintenance and repair.

The basic software will be able to call on three universal knowledge bases arranged as elements of the knowledge-base management system. The particular elements will give basic words in everyday use, basic sentence patterns and scripts, dictionaries and sentence-construction rules for various languages, and various other components related to natural language. The systems knowledge base will include specifications for the system itself, a language manual component, and a program module component (containing much-used programs). The application knowledge base will include a basic program component, a computer architecture component, and a component for VLSI design. It will be possible to use three categories of programming languages with a fifth-generation computer (see Figure 2.7).

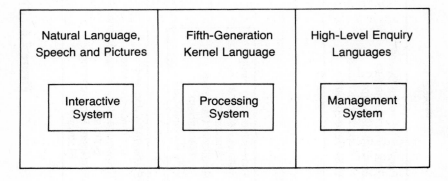

Figure 2.7   Categories of Application Systems

Only the kernel programming language will be used to program the computer, and only this language will be directly supported by the knowledge-base machines and by the problem-solving and inference machines. The aim is that the kernel language will be a problem-solving language based on predicate logic, as is PROLOG. In such a language, a program comprises logic statements of a restricted form *(clauses)*, and program execution is in effect a logical deduction from the program clauses. Other languages (eg enquiry languages for knowledge bases) will be implemented in terms of the kernel language. It is not envisaged that all users of fifth-generation computers will need to learn languages such as PROLOG or LISP (see Languages, below). Instead, it is intended that future computer users will be able to interact with machines by means of natural language.

Languages

PROLOG (PROgramming in LOGic) has been adopted as the effective kernel language for fifth-generation computers, ie it is likely that the main fifth-generation language to be used in computers in the 1990s will be enhanced dialects of PROLOG. In PROLOG, use is made of a form of basic mathematical logic, called *resolution,* developed by Professor John Robinson of Syracuse University in the US. This approach allows problems to be solved by means of a series of logical inferences (similar to how expert systems use deductive reasoning, see Chapter 4).

We have already mentioned the use of 'clauses' as restricted-form logic statements. The basic unit of a PROLOG program is a *Horn clause* which can be either a direct statement (or *assertion*), such as:

Fred works 38 hours a week

or an *implication,* such as

if x works z hours *and* earns p/hour *then* x is paid y

From such assertions and implications, it is possible to produce a specification of an information processing task or to define database search requirements. The specification can serve as a program procedure or as a relational database enquiry. Hence PROLOG bridges the gap between a specification and a programming language and also between a programming and a database enquiry language. Moreover, formal techniques can be used to prove the correctness of a PROLOG specification. Since it resembles the natural way of expressing problems, PROLOG is relatively easy to learn, even by children.

PROLOG is also being used in Europe and elsewhere for various practical purposes. For instance, the London-based LPA Ltd is offering PROLOG implementations for several microcomputers and for DEC VAX superminicomputers. Micro Prolog is offered for microcomputers configured around the Zilog Z80 and running under Digital Research's CP/M version 2.2. The VAX implementation, termed MPROLOG, originates from the Budapest Institute for Coordination of Computer Techniques (MPROLOG was introduced in 1980). The first hosts for this language were mainframes from Siemens and IBM. At the London fifth-generation conference staged by SPL International, various successful PROLOG applications were cited: for example, scientific information retrieval, software generation and analysis, computer architecture design, and CAD for buildings and pharmaceutical research.

There is a clear sense in which PROLOG is a proven language, particularly well suited – because it is written in terms of relations – to the task of manipulating knowledge databases. Alex Goodall, managing director of the new company Expert Systems, has emphasised that PROLOG provides the facilities required for intelligence programs: 'Anyone new to the AI field would be unwise to go for anything else as it is easier to use than LISP and more powerful than the other alternative Pop-2'. Expert Systems is aiming to sell 200 microcomputer versions of PROLOG by introducing interpreters for 16-bit machines.

LISP (LISt Programming), a more limited example of logical programming, was developed in 1960 by a pioneer of AI, Professor John McCarthy of the Massachusetts Institute of Technology. The basic program structure of LISP is a *list* or *string*. Pure LISP (sometimes called S-LISP) represents lists within parentheses. For example, to add two numbers (x and y) together, the LISP statement would be:

(PLUS X Y)

where PLUS is the function that adds two numbers together. The basic structure can be difficult to understand for complex functions, and so easier versions of LISP have been developed.

The LISP language, able to specify other languages, is sometimes referred to as a *metalanguage*. For instance, it has been used to generate the LOGO language for educational systems, and also languages which enable algebraic expressions to be evaluated directly in the form that would normally be expressed by a mathematician. PROLOG can be used to perform many LISP-type operations.

Logic programming languages such as PROLOG, PROLOG derivatives and LISP are likely to be used extensively in fifth-generation computers. Again, it can be emphasised that one fifth-generation objective is to allow computer users to be less-well-versed in programming languages, ie to be able to communicate with the computer using natural language.

With artificial intelligence increasingly finding its way into the commercial marketplace, a significant hardware market is starting to emerge. There is growing competition between vendors offering machines that run LISP, now regarded, as we have seen, as a key AI language. Xerox, for example, has used LISP for years for advanced computer science research and development, and the company now offers several internally-developed LISP machines, the Xerox 1100 scientific information processor (the 'Dolphin'), the Dandelion/1108 and the Dorado/1132. At the same time, various other companies have produced LISP-based machines: for example the LM-2 (from Symbolics Inc) and the Lisp Machine (from Lisp Machine Inc).

Languages such as PROLOG and LISP have had high exposure in the media, and with PROLOG deemed to be the kernel language for fifth-generation systems the surrounding publicity is hardly surprising. At the same time, other languages suitable for fifth-generation architectures are being developed. For example, recent research reports from Japan, whilst giving most attention to PROLOG and LISP, also consider DURAL (a modal extension of PROLOG) and VALID (a high-level functional language for data flow machines).

DURAL exploits aspects of modal logic to classify the *clauses*. With this approach, DURAL has a number of characteristic features:

— modal symbols are introduced to discriminate between clauses;

— the relative Horn clause represents the clause containing executable predicates;

— the unit resolution, as well as input resolution, is adopted to facilitate debugging.

Shigeki Goto (1981) considers aspects of modal logic and the use of modal symbols, and describes such features as the relative Horn clause and unit resolution. (DURAL has been implemented in MACLISP and run on a DEC System 20.)

VALID (VALue IDentification language) is a high-level language designed for programming on data flow machines (Amamiya, 1981). The basic design concept is that VALID semantics support programming based on the functional approach (similar to LISP), while the syntax offers programmers the conventions to write programs in a style akin to Algol.

A version of VALID has already been designed as a basic language for programming support on data flow machine systems, including the data flow machine software simulator in the Japanese fifth-generation programme. The compiler generates codes for two types of data flow machines: the large-scale scientific calculation oriented data flow processor system, and the list-processing oriented data flow machine. Thus, VALID has specialised forms (VALID-N and VALID-S) for numerical calculation and symbolic manipulation respectively.

Another language of interest is occam (termed a fifth-generation language) from Inmos. In late-1982 it appeared in the marketplace as an evaluation kit aimed at companies keen to experiment with concurrent programming. The aim is to launch a fully-fledged occam in 1983. This language can be used to design entire systems, and there is a strong bias towards the treatment of parallel processing systems. By the time Inmos launches its Transputer computer-on-a-chip in 1984, a full occam development sys-

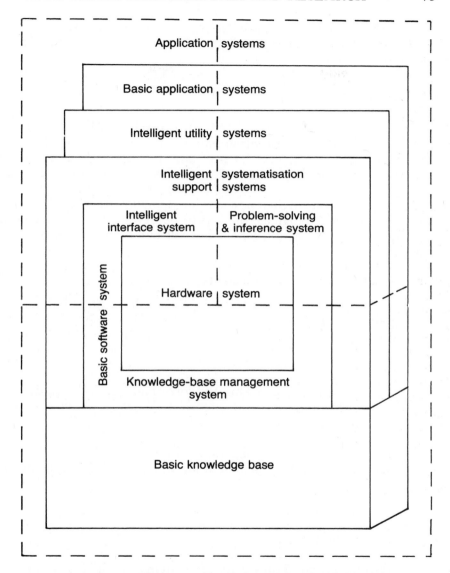

Figure 2.8   Fifth-Generation Computer Software System
(Source: *Proceedings of the International Conference on Fifth-Generation Computer Systems,* 19-22 October, 1981, JIPDEC)

tem will be available as one of the first system development languages for new computer design. Iann Barron, managing director of Inmos, has suggested that the company will be able to use the Transputer to overtake the Japanese in the race to fifth-generation systems. (Fawcett, 1982, describes some of the important features of occam.)

The various languages discussed – the kernel language PROLOG, LISP (another logic programming language), DURAL (a PROLOG derivative), VALID (for data flow machines), occam (the Inmos innovation), etc – are by no means an exhaustive list. They merely indicate a few selected areas of importance. The software scene is one of flux: new systems demands are forcing new languages and new language dialects to be developed. It is likely that many fifth-generation languages will emerge over the next decade.

Fifth-Generation Software Elements

Various features of fifth-generation software have already been highlighted. Partly by way of summary, it is worth emphasising the constituent elements of the software envisaged for fifth-generation computers (these elements are shown in Figure 2.8). The various constituent elements can be identified:

— *basic software system*. This, the core of all systems, includes the problem-solving and inference system, a knowledge-base management system, and an intelligent interface system (these systems are seen as corresponding respectively to the problem-solving and inference machine, the knowledge-base management machine, and the intelligent interface machine);

— *intelligent systematisation support systems*. These are the group of systems which, in designing optimum information processing systems for various applications, will be in a position to reduce the amount of human effort needed in system design. Three support systems are included: for intelligent programming, for handling a knowledge base, and for designing VLSI chips and architectures;

— *intelligent utility systems*. These provide various functions to facilitate use of the system itself. They include a system to ease the transfer of stored programs and databases for commercial machines to a target machine, a system explanation system, and a trouble diagnosis and maintenance system;

— *basic knowledge bases*. These are employable for the applications systems that the user will operate. The general knowledge base is analogous to human common sense; and

---

Machine translation system

Question-answering time

Applied speech understanding system

— Phonetic (voice inputting) typewriter: Should handle 10,000 words, possess a meaning analysing function, be capable of correcting errors in speech by itself, and output sentences easy to understand

— Speech-responding system: Should handle 10,000 words, be able to grasp the meaning of responses and thus be capable of natural conversation

— Speaker identifies system: Should be able to handle a few hundred people or more and identify speakers within a practical interval of time.

Applied picture and image understanding system

— This system should structurally store about 100,000 pieces of information in picture and image form so as to be usable for knowledge information processing

---

Table 4   Themes and Targets for Basic Applications Systems (see also Table 2)
(Source: *Proceedings of the International Conference on Fifth-Generation Computer Systems,* 19-22 October 1981, JIPDEC)

other knowledge bases will carry knowledge about systems and applications;

— *basic application systems*. Various types of application system can be cited (see Tables 2 and 4), and various systems can be regarded as examples of knowledge information processing application systems: CAE/CAD systems, CAI systems, OA systems, and intelligent robots.

KNOWLEDGE INFORMATION PROCESSING

Human intelligence typically relies upon building up a collection of *knowledge* and then applying reasons to *infer* what course of action should be adopted. Research into artificial intelligence has already yielded a range of *expert systems* (Chapter 4) which use knowledge-refining techniques to distil human knowledge into computer systems.

To develop an expert system, it is necessary for the human developer to talk to experts in the specialisation (or *domain*) to be covered, with the special logic programming languages (see above) used to represent the knowledge in a systematic form. The aim in such cases is to develop a system which, when complete, can be consulted as if it were a human expert. The earliest expert systems typically assisted in medical diagnosis, geological prospecting and biochemical analysis.

An expert systems program will typically generate statements such as:

If x is true and y is true then there is a z%
chance that m is true.

In other words, the human user is given an answer (eg medical symptoms are fed in for a diagnosis) and the expert system gives an indication of how likely the answer is to be correct. The typical expert system statement thus is a quantified way of expressing reasoning, and as the system is programmed in a way that represents human knowledge and inference, its 'code' is easy to understand. Ideally, the expert system, appropriately questioned, can provide answers and explain how they are reached.

Knowledge representation and processing are regarded as the heart of fifth-generation computers. In fact, expert systems are sometimes wrongly identified directly with fifth-generation systems. However, expert systems have been working – with a degree of success that is open to debate – for many years, whereas we will be lucky to see true fifth-generation computers in the 1980s. What is central to the two types of systems is the notion of knowledge information processing: this idea has long been at the core of expert systems, and the fifth-generation computer is sometimes known as the Knowledge Information Processing System (KIPS).

We have seen that the hardware for fifth-generation computer systems will comprise three major functional components (from the standpoint of the basic software interface): the problem-solving and inference component, the knowledge-base management component and the intelligent man/machine interface component. The knowledge-base management component functions include mechanisms for retrieving and storing information, a key element in knowledge manipulation; and the knowledge-base management component and the inference control component together comprise the knowledge-base machine. The role of this machine is summarised as follows:

— the machine holds a large amount of information that is well structured for each access to information items;

— when the knowledge-base machine receives a demand from the inference machine, it retrieves knowledge items and conveys them to the inference machine;

— when the knowledge-base machine receives knowledge data items from the inference machine, it integrates them into the knowledge base.

Makoto Amamiya et al (1981) discuss the design of architectures for knowledge-base mechanisms.

The development of facilities – architectures, languages, software, etc – for knowledge manipulation is a key element in research towards fifth-generation. It is largely by the efficient high-speed processing of knowledge that fifth-generation computers will be recognised.

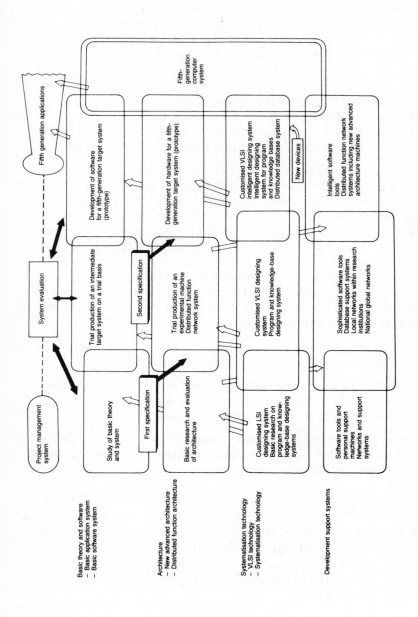

Figure 2.9   How R and D is to Progress in the Fifth-Generation Programme
(Source: *Proceedings of the International Conference on Fifth-Generation Computer Systems,*
19-22 October, 1981, JIPDEC)

R AND D PROJECTS

The Japanese Ministry of Trade and Industry, MITI, is funding ICOT to research fifth-generation systems under four groups. These groups, or working parties, are devoted to Architecture, Core Language, Natural Language, and Theory and Knowledge Base. The MITI expenditure over the first three years is expected to reach about £30 million. (For the response of the Alvey Committee to this scheme, see Chapter 6.) Efforts are being made in Japan to free certain company researchers, working under the ICOT programme, from the pressures of company work.

Various research and development projects have already been mentioned in this chapter. It is worth listing the important themes in R and D for the fifth-generation programme (see Table 5). Efforts have been made to indicate how the various projects are to be implemented (Figure 2.9). It may be assumed that this conceptual approach will be modified as fifth-generation research and development unfolds over the next decade.

SUMMARY

This chapter has surveyed the main features of fifth-generation computer systems, as currently conceived (mainly in Japan). Some indication is given of the social impulse behind the generation of a new range of computers, before examining such system features as hardware, integrated circuits, architectures, software, languages, knowledge information processing, and the range of running research and development projects.

The fifth-generation research programme is still, in 1983, in its infancy, and many of the theoretical objectives may be out-of-reach – at least by the stipulated prototype year of 1991. At the same time, we may expect the fifth-generation research programme to yield many fruits, not least in the realms of artificial intelligence (Chapter 3) and expert systems (Chapter 4).

Another consequence of the Japanese initiative is that other technological countries are being stimulated to respond, as a necessary condition of national economic survival. In these circumstances there could be many unexpected consequences for national computer industries. And the outcome is quite unpredictable. The present chapter has largely profiled Japanese intentions, but initiatives in the US and Europe could be highly significant for the realisation of the fifth-generation features profiled above.

Basic application systems	Machine translation system Question-answering system Applied speech-understanding system Applied picture- and image- understanding system Applied problem-solving system
Basic software systems	Knowledge-base management system Problem-solving and inference system Intelligent interface system
New advanced architecture	Logic programming machine Functional machine Relational algebra machine Abstract data type support machine Data flow machine Innovative von Neumann machine

Distributed function architecture	Distributed function architecture
	Network architecture
	Database machine
	High-speed numerical computation
	    machine
	High-level man-machine communication
	    system

VLSI technology	VLSI architecture Intelligent VLSI CAD system

Systematisation technology	Intelligent programming system
	Knowledge-base design system
	Systematisation technology for
	    computer architecture
	Database and distributed database
	    system

Development supporting technology	Development support system

Table 5   Themes in R and D for Fifth-Generation Computers
(Source: *Proceedings of the International Conference on Fifth-Generation Computer Systems,* 19-22 October, 1981, JIPDEC)

3 Artificial Intelligence

INTRODUCTION

One of the most significant features of fifth-generation research is the new emphasis on the importance of artificial intelligence (AI). Problem-solving and inference-making, key elements in new-generation computers, will draw heavily on established AI work (see below). And such fifth-generation concerns as the intelligent man/machine interface will depend upon progress in such traditional AI fields as pattern recognition and the understanding of natural language. This is not to say that *all* AI topics will be equally relevant to the development of fifth-generation computers, only that the new systems will not emerge without significant AI input.

This is an unprecedented situation in the history of computing. Until recently, artificial intelligence was seen as a poor relative of mainstream topics in computer research, generating excitement in some circles but often seen as an expensive and fruitless line of enquiry. Today AI research is increasingly regarded as central in the development of new-generation systems.

Part of the problem in developing *artificial* intelligence is that we are not at all sure how to define *natural* intelligence. Efforts to quantify intelligence in human beings – for example, using Binet IQ tests – have yielded limited results, showing correlations between performance in tests and certain types of professional competence, but only crudely distinguishing between different *types* of intelligence (arithmetic, verbal, spatial, philosophic, etc). We have a view (or an image) of intelligence but have difficulty in defining it in the formal terms that are essential for computer systems. In fact the formal requirements of AI systems are having a salutory impact on research in human (and animal) psychology: there is an unprecedented emphasis on *rigour* in framing concepts, categories, research programmes, individual experiments, etc.

Various definitions of intelligence have accumulated over the years. Alfred Binet himself thought that the concept related to 'comprehension, invention, direction and criticism, or judgement'. David Wechsler suggested that intelligence is 'the aggregate or global capacity of an individual to act purposefully, to think rationally and to deal effectively with his environment'. And the psychologist William Stern viewed it as 'the general capacity of an individual consciously to adjust his thinking to new requirements and a general adaptability to new problems and conditions'. Sceptics have suggested that intelligence is the ability to do IQ tests, an interpretation that is nicely enhanced by the fact that at least one recent paper has focused on the ability of computers to do intelligence tests: Mason (1982) has discussed how computers can tackle a standard intelligence test by using the calculus of finite differences.

Apart from the difficulties in formalising *natural* intelligence, many people still find the notion of artificial intelligence conceptually odd. Margaret Boden (1977) relates her experiences with a Moscow taxi-driver when she was visiting an AI conference: on learning of the nature of the conference, he 'roared with laughter and made the "crazy-sign" against his forehead; nor did he stop doing this, his shoulders shaking, until he had dropped us at our destination some five minutes later'. To this man, intelligent artefacts offered no threat, 'just comic relief'. We may expect such types of responses to become less frequent as artificial intelligence develops as a main element in fifth-generation computers and other high-technology products.

The AI world traditionally needed vast computer power to achieve rather unimpressive results. A typical example is in early efforts to achieve computer vision: a simple task in 'image understanding' took about 3 hours of large machine time to accomplish, and even with special hardware about 30 minutes was required. Any effective vision system, however, requires that recognition tasks be performed in a fraction of a second. With the emergence of new technologies and a vast range of software, the tardiness of early AI processing is now a thing of the past. Increasingly, modern researchers recognise the importance of AI elements in computer systems. One consequence is the development of *knowledge engineering* (see below), a new discipline aimed in part at building intellectual competence into expert and other types of AI systems. Thus, one of the founding fathers of the Japanese strategy in computing. Tosio Kitagawa, observed in 1980 that 'when program logics can be adaptive to data assigned there is the opportunity to turn information flows through knowledge bases, into intelligence of a broad nature'.

Developments in artificial intelligence are proceeding simultaneously on several fronts (some of these are represented by the headings in the present chapter), and these have a convergent tendency. Different AI concerns tend to merge, to grow increasingly inter-dependent: hence, memory mechanisms underlie knowledge engineering which in turn relates directly to such activities as language understanding and learning in the real world. This chapter profiles some of the more important areas in AI research without making any effort to quantify their likely impact on the fifth-generation programme. What is clear is that any fruits of AI research will quickly be seen as relevant to the design of new-generation computer systems.

THE NATURE OF AI

Artificial intelligence is part of computer science, but a part that tends to focus on programs. Indeed, some AI researchers seem curiously indifferent to hardware. Margaret Boden comments, perhaps rather too blandly (in *Artificial Intelligence and Natural Man*): 'One thing, however, is certain: artificial intelligence is not the study of computers. Computers are metallic machines of intrinsic interest to electronic engineers but not, as such, to many others. So if you are not enamored of tin cans, you need not fear to meet any in this book'. The tin-can image of computers is not, however, universal among AI researchers: some, for instance, work with real robots as well as with simulated robots. A fancy AI program may be elegant and intellectually satisfying but it is no use for any practical purpose if there is no way of running it. And the practical character of AI is nicely encapsulated by M. L. Minsky:

'Artificial intelligence is the science of making machines do things that would require intelligence if done by men'.

Any particular emphasis in AI research is likely to depend upon the preoccupations of the researcher. Some workers in the field are mainly interested in the psychologies of living creatures. Here AI is seen as a means of throwing light on, for example, human conversation or learning abilities. Some aim simply to build clever toys, such as the American Cubot, a robot (with fingers, eye and brain) that can solve any scrambled Rubik cube in less than four minutes. And other AI researchers work in the mainstream of commercial computer manufacture, concerned mainly with the development of successful commercial products.

Most fifth-generation workers with involvement in AI topics belong in the last category. Theoretical AI findings are relevant to any area of interest, but the main thrust behind fifth-generation research is to generate practical systems that will have a beneficial impact on society, on the viability of industrial economies and on the quality of life. In the light of the seeming disinterest in hardware on the part of some AI workers, it is worth emphasising that the fifth-generation research programme is intended to yield a range of practical, and far-reaching, consequences. If it were otherwise, national governments would be less interested in finding the vast sums necessary for investment funding.

COMPUTERS AND PSYCHOLOGY

By 1960 it was obvious that computer developments would profoundly affect views about human psychology. It was already clear that the new electronic devices could do many of the things that were formerly the sole prerogative of human beings and other intelligent creatures. For instance, computers could learn, store and recall information, solve problems, take decisions, and carry out simple reasoning tasks. Newell et al (1958) and other researchers were already beginning to recast the traditional psychological questions in terms of computer analogies. In a discernible move away from stimulus-response (S-R) behaviourism, a new interest was developing in internal mental processes and structures which could now be described in programming terms. This work was quickly seen to be relevant to the building of new artificial systems that could mimic or simulate certain aspects of human psychology, including intelligence.

The new theoretical schemes were so powerful that it became reasonable to suppose that the human mental apparatus was not merely analogous to a computer but was in fact a type of computer itself, a system of staggering complexity which had nonetheless evolved as an information-processing machine. Earl Hunt (1971) asked 'What kind of a computer is man?' and began the task of describing a computing system that 'thinks like a man'. This type of consideration bears directly on main elements in the current fifth-generation research programme. By the early-1970s it was becoming clear that computers were telling us more about the human mind, and new psychological concepts were enlarging our vision of what computers would become. Researchers were already erecting the conceptual framework within which the ambitious fifth-generation research programme would be launched.

In 1956, Miller published a paper which encouraged the development of an information-processing model for human psychology, and later he and co-workers suggested, as an alternative to traditional behaviourism, a cognitive approach based on the idea that the unit of behaviour is a *plan,* a behaviour-generating system similar to the feedback loops used in computers. This suggests that man is an active processor of information, capable of initiative but working according to procedures that could be examined in terms of computer models. Neisser (1967) proposed a specific information-processing model comprising specific memory stores and processes, and by 1980 Allport was able to declare that '. . . the advent of Artificial Intelligence is the single most important development in the history of psychology'.

Scientists in the 1950s were beginning to use ideas in neurophysiology to develop theories on simple learning and pattern recognition (this latter being relevant to the future development of intelligent man/machine interfaces in fifth-generation systems). What we have seen is a conflux of influences – from psychology, biology, cybernetics, etc – shaping the emerging character of artificial intelligence.

A main aim of fifth generation is to make machines more 'humanlike' in their responses and processes. Work in cognitive psychology, itself shaped by computer influences over the last three decades, is helping researchers to bridge the gap between human and machine processes. Conversely, it is through the development of computer science that we are learning to understand human mental processes (and those of other animals) in terms of systems, programs, plans, structures, etc: it is through the development of computer science, leavened by accumulating psychological insights, that we are learning to build cognitive capacities into artefacts. The bulk of AI topics (most of the headings in this chapter) belong also in the branches of modern psychology dealing with cognition. It may not be too fanciful to suggest that the emerging fifth-generation computers will have cognitive psychologies (see below).

COGNITIVE FACTORS

Some of the most innovative computer scientists have emphasised how insights in a biological area (eg brain function) may aid development in computer science. Von Neumann, for instance, approached the human nervous system from a mathematical point of view, suggesting that the system is part digital, part analogue and part hybrid. He also concluded that the nervous system transmits data in (almost periodic) trains of pulses with frequencies of the order of 50 to 100 pulses per second, much as in a frequency-modulated signalling system. The coding used in this means of transmitting information has been dubbed the 'machine language' of the nervous system.

Von Neumann also attempted a quantitative comparison between the basic organs of the human nervous system and the components of a computer. Limited to experience with first-generation computers, he nonetheless stimulated an approach to machine intelligence which was to prove immensely fertile. One of his conclusions – of obvious relevance to fifth-generation machines – was that the high performance achievable in natural processing machines would depend upon a parallel processing capability. The implication is that, for artificial systems to approach human systems in processing power, a parallel architecture with appropriate software is essential. It is ironic that a move away from von Neumann architectures is seen to characterise fifth-generation developments when he clearly envisaged the need for parallel, rather than sequential, processing in high-performance systems.

The various brain functions that can be usefully modelled in artificial systems together make up the mental capability of the individual. Not all the functions represent *cognitive* elements. For example, efforts are being made to model emotional dispositions and attitudes. These are not of direct interest to cognitive psychologists or to researchers in fifth generation. The principle cognitive elements in AI, most of which have immediate relevance to new-generation systems, are such things as memory, learning, problem-solving, inference (or deduction), pattern recognition (or perception), decision-making, language understanding and game playing.

It is obvious that cognitive considerations will increasingly affect computer design. Allen (1982) has drawn attention to many aspects of modern computing that have cognitive relevance ('There is a cognitive component even in simple keying tasks . . .'). This sort of consideration relates specifically to man/machine interaction, again of interest to workers in fifth generation. Allen considers such aspects as short- and long-term memory, problem-solving and empirical studies relating to directing a computer's actions (through database access languages, command languages, menus and trees, natural language, etc), to cognitive factors in programming, problem-solving, document preparation and other aspects. A main conclusion is that 'as computers and software become sophisticated, the relevance of cognitive factors seems likely to increase'.

The nature of AI interest in fifth-generation systems is such that topics with a cognitive significance are directly relevant to the research programme. Already the cognitive implications of such tasks as programming, using command languages, and accessing a database have been studied in detail. Research into specific cognitive areas will be seen to have increasing relevance to human psychology and to the development of new-generation computer systems. The rest of this chapter is devoted to profiling some of the cognitive topics that are at the heart of AI and which will increasingly affect the design of new hardware, system architectures, software and programming languages.

MEMORY MECHANISMS

The storing of information is essential to most of the intelligent tasks carried out by artificial and biological systems. And information has not only to be stored – on a short- or long-term basis – but manipulated (processed) and retrieved when necessary. Speedy retrieval of information is necessary when a computer has to react in a rapidly changing real-time situation. Or knowledge may need to be accessed months or years after it was first injected into the system. In the sophisticated AI systems of the future there will be a need for numerous files of reference data – to provide, for instance, a world model, self-awareness structures, etc, on a day-to-day basis. Virtually all the cognitive tasks presuppose either the collecting, processing or accessing of stored information. Effective memory (information-storage) mechanisms are essential to the efficient intelligent operation of both biological and artificial systems.

Memory in artificial (and biological) systems depends upon the effectiveness of such things as passive and active systems, specific memory-element designs, coding techniques and philosophies, retrieval routes, the extent of content-addressable memory, and storage capacities in buffers and other subsystems. In one memory model highlighted by Winograd (1975), the information-storage element is shown as a set of independent components controlled by a central processing unit that calls up information when required and encodes specific input information to memory cells. This process involves 'search' and 'active message processing', where each memory element may have 'the power to do its own computations on a message that is sent to the memory elements, and each element can decide independently what action it should take'. This arrangement is seen as essentially similar to human memory, where specific memory items are linked with others in a network.

A system with *passive* memory allows items of information to be stored in specific locations which can be accessed sequentially (like running through a tape recording until a desired item is located) or by random access means (where preliminary processing defines the 'address' of the item). By contrast, *active* memory elements are connected in a network, and information can be retrieved in various ways (content-addressable methods being the simplest).

In some computer models, eg Reitman's (1970) Waiting-Room

Model, input processing is represented in short-term memory: such models imply a close similarity between the relevant processes in computers and human beings (in fact, shortcomings in the Reitman model are suggested by the non-equivalence between certain machine and human outputs). Some models – for example, Feigenbaum's EPAM (Elementary Perceiver and Memoriser) and Hintzman's SAL (Stimulus and Association Learner) – are seen as representing limited subsets of memory functions. The Feigenbaum program, for instance, is regarded as an early example of how a cognitive process can be effectively modelled.

EPAM shows how it may be that we can forget something for a long time, yet remember it when suitably prompted: here, information is never destroyed but may be hidden for a time, one memory masking another. It is also interesting that EPAM can behave in ways that were not 'programmed in': the program carries no interference routines, but in certain circumstances the acquisition of a new association can interfere with the production of an older one.

The notion of limited-capacity processing in short-term human memory has also been widely postulated. In this connection, efforts have been made to develop the idea of a 'central executive processor', so extending the analogy between natural and artificial memory. And stored data, as we have seen, is increasingly being viewed, in artificial systems, as *knowledge* (see Knowledge Engineering, below). In one view (Bond, 1981), 'the history of machine intelligence can be viewed as the development of knowledge representation methods', an idea that is intimately linked to the development of expert systems (Chapter 4) and other AI configurations. Here the *rule,* representing a particular fragment of knowledge, is a key concept. Various possible system organisations can be used to determine how rules are used in the execution of a program.

The development of computer models of memory, knowledge- or rule-based systems shows how appropriate information storage mechanisms can be built into artefacts. The various performance requirements of fifth-generation computers suggest the need for a wide range of new information-storage mechanisms. Often the designs will be influenced by insights into naturally-occurring memory systems, ie memories in human beings and other animals.

KNOWLEDGE ENGINEERING

Data processing, in one form or another, has always been at the heart of computer activity, and this will remain true with fifth-generation systems. At the same time, there is a significant shift of emphasis in the terminology. For the first time, it is regarded as realistic to see computers as handling *knowledge* as well as *data* or *information. Knowledge* suggests *understanding* and *intelligence,* characteristic features of emerging fifth-generation systems in their gradual approach to 'humanlike' performance.

The manipulation of knowledge is a central purpose of expert systems and many other computer configurations influenced by AI developments. One aim is that knowledge from human experts be fed into artificial systems for subsequent manipulation and retrieval. The inference capabilities of the system allow the information to be used in such a way that generalisations, associations, conclusions, etc, can be achieved in response to human users wanting advice or processed information in a specialist area. (The transfer of *all* human knowledge to computer systems will be a daunting task: in 1981 it was suggested that human knowledge was expanding at the rate of 200 million words per hour.) The development of techniques and systems for the automatic manipulation of knowledge has, in recent years, been dubbed *knowledge engineering,* a discipline that draws on work in various fields (such as cognitive psychology, information theory, computer science and artificial intelligence). It is important to emphasise the relevance of AI to knowledge engineering.

In artificial intelligence, *data structures* and *interpretive procedures* can be combined in a program to produce 'knowledgeable' behaviour. To aid knowledge representation, several classes of data structures have been designed for storing information in computer programs, and appropriate inference procedures allow the intelligent manipulation of the data structures. We may emphasise that the data structures, in themselves, are not knowledge: rather, knowledge may be recognised as the effective use of data structures in a program.

Various efforts have been made to identify the types of knowledge that might need to be represented in an AI system. (This is partly a matter for cognitive psychology.) Barr and Feigenbaum

(1981) have identified the following kinds of knowledge:

— *objects*. Knowledge often relates to facts about objects in the world, so there should be some way of representing the categories and descriptions of objects;

— *events*. Actions and events are key elements in knowledge. Events need to be encoded, and it may also be necessary to define time sequences and cause-and-effect relations;

— *performance*. Some knowledge concerns skills, ie how to do things. Most cognitive behaviour (eg composing sentences, solving theorems) involves performance knowledge;

— *meta-knowledge*. This is 'knowledge about what we know', eg knowledge about the extent of our knowledge or about our performance limitations.

The manipulation of these various types of knowledge – and there may be others – in AI systems can serve a variety of practical goals (such as recognising physical objects in the real world, answering questions in a specialist subject, and controlling an intelligent robot). Knowledge manipulation can aid the acquisition of further knowledge (ie learning), retrieving information relevant to the particular problem and reasoning about the various facts to reach a solution.

There are problems associated with these various activities. The acquisition of new knowledge can interfere with existing data structures; accessing 'relevant' information can be theoretically, as well as practically, problematic; and, similarly, the mechanics of inference, not fully understood in human beings, are difficult to structure into AI programs (there are, for example, many different types of reasoning: formal, procedural, reasoning by analogy, generalisation, abstraction, meta-level reasoning, etc). It is the business of knowledge engineering to address itself to these types of questions. Again, Barr and Feigenbaum (1981) highlight some of the characteristics of knowledge representation schemes that have been used to describe different formalisms.

Questions concerning the *scope* and *grain size* of a representation focus on the detail in which objects and events are represented, and on what portion of the external world can be represented in the particular system. And the character of the *mapping* of objects and events in the world into some internal encoding can be examined (is the mapping 'easy, natural, psychologically valid, and the like'?).

It has also been found that the choice of the primitive attributes of the domain used to build up facts in the knowledge base can strongly affect the effectiveness of the knowledge representation scheme. For example, it is possible to encode a simple fact in many different ways, and in certain cases the system may be confused in looking for particular structures in order to retrieve relevant facts. This type of difficulty relates to the question of *indeterminacy and semantic primitives*. Other questions relate to *modularity and understanding* (for example, can individual data structures be added or deleted more or less independently of the remainder of the database?), *explicit knowledge and flexibility* (what knowledge can the programmer access and what knowledge is built in?), and *declarative versus procedural representations* (concerning such features as system economy, completeness, ease of coding and understandability).

The concept of *rule,* representing a particular fragment of knowledge, is central to knowledge engineering. This has been represented as:

$$\text{pattern} \longrightarrow \text{action}$$

Here the *pattern* is regarded as a conjunction of primitive perceptual *tests,* the right-hand side being a set of primitive actions. One common form of the database is a set of data objects which are attribute-value lists, in which case the tests are the values of attributes, and the actions alter such values or carry out input/output tasks. Each rule, highly relevant to the organisation of expert and other AI systems, can be put into expressions along the lines of:

> if the value of attribute x is . . . and the value of attribute y is . . . , then the value of attribute z is . . .

The set of rules is regarded as comprising the knowledge of the system. Various different types of system organisation are available to determine how the rules are employed when the program is executed. The entire operation of the program may be depicted as a sequence of rule evocations. (More is said about this in Chapter 4.)

Developments in knowledge engineering are central to the emergence of sophisticated expert systems and other types of AI configuration, in fifth generation or elsewhere. Already progress in this area is yielding new approaches to the handling of human knowledge in various specialist fields. Most commonly we see papers focusing on medical diagnosis or chemical analysis, but, in principle, no field is immune to a 'knowledge engineering analysis' with a view to configuring AI systems capable of learning, inference, and other cognitive tasks. Lee et al (1982) have shown the relevance of AI and knowledge engineering to work in the social sciences, and this is only one example from an accumulating literature.

PROBLEM-SOLVING

Problem-solving, at the heart of much AI research, may be regarded as a generalised concept that can attain specific focus in many different areas: for example, computation, language processing, theorem proving, inference drawing and game playing. The various approaches to computer chess are often cited as exemplifying various problem-solving questions. Two broad ways of tackling problems – algorithm and heuristic – are also often illustrated by reference to game playing and other cognitive activities in the real world. (Broadly, *algorithms* are well-defined procedures that guarantee a solution to a problem; *heuristics* are empirical rules or strategies, akin to 'rule of thumb'.) The complexity of many problem-solving activities makes the algorithm approach impractical: the progressive development of heuristic techniques – for problem-solving and other activities – may be regarded as allowing computers to evolve a more 'humanlike' intelligence. A problem-solving capability is seen as central to the concept of fifth-generation computers.

An early heuristic program, a major step forward for artificial intelligence, was developed in 1956 by Newell and Simon as a joint project of the Rand Corporation and the Carnegie Institute of Technology. In their heuristic approach, these researchers wanted to understand how a mathematician 'is able to prove a theorem even though he does not know when he starts how, or if, he is going to succeed'. In this context, heuristics became identified with processes 'that may solve a given problem, but offer no guarantee of doing so'.

The 1956 program, the Logic Theorist, had as its problem domain the proof of theorems in the propositional calculus, with both the axioms and theorems taken from *Principia Mathematica* by Bertrand Russell and Alfred North Whitehead. In fact the Logic Theorist succeeded in proving thirty-eight of the first fifty-two theorems in Chapter 2 of that seminal work. The program operates by reasoning backwards from the theorem to be proved to the initial axioms and given theorems. Barr and Feigenbaum (1981) describe in detail how the Logic Theorist works.

Many of the ideas underlying the Logic Theorist were developed – by Newell, Shaw and Simon, starting in 1957 – to form the General Problem Solver (GPS). GPS was developed over more than a decade, eventually incorporating a powerful general strategy for the solution of a wide range of problems. This problem-solving program was significant in that it was the first to separate its general problem-solving methods from knowledge specific to the type of task being handled. The problem-solving part of the system provided no information about the task; task-dependent knowledge was compiled in data structures to form a task environment. Overall, the program simulated the general strategies used by human beings in problem-solving, and it could be applied to problems in chess, in logic, in theorem proving, etc. Ernst and Newell (1969) (and later Newell and Simon in 1972) asked people to solve problems and to explain what they were doing as they worked, then extracted from the reports a general strategy for incorporation into the program.

It is important to emphasise the *general* character of GPS. The program was intended 'to model generality in problem solving' using techniques of heuristic search and the strategy of means-ends analysis. GPS was tested on eleven types of very different problems – 'missionaries and cannibals', mathematical integration, theorem-proving, parsing sentences, letter-series completion, etc. In solving these problems, GPS generated goal structures that did not always resemble those produced by human beings. However, the GPS process in general resembles human problem-solving methods: simple subgoals are first set as likely to lead to a solution, and then the means-ends analysis process applies the relevant heuristic method to reach the subgoal. The analysis uses given data and carries out appropriate transformations much as a human being does in tackling a problem. If the applied heuristic fails, another is tried and another – until the solution is achieved or the attempt abandoned.

GPS was only able to solve relatively simple problems. Its generality was purchased at the expense of efficiency: special-purpose problem-solvers were better at finding solutions in their defined domains. At the same time, GPS was never intended to be a high-performance program. Ernst and Newell (1969) instead saw it as yielding 'a series of lessons that give a more perfect view of the nature of problem solving and what is required to construct processes that accomplish it'. GPS*was the first program to embody the *planning* strategy for problem-solving, and other programs using this basic approach – in which a simplified version of the problem is used as a model, details being filled in later – were to follow. For example, Boden (1977) describes four planning programs (GPS, ABSTRIPS, NOAH, and BUILD) of increasing power.

What we have seen is the emergence of various techniques (usually heuristic) that can be programmed for the solution of problems. In the development of a generalised problem-solving capacity central to the requirements of fifth-generation systems, GPS is seen as a seminal program. Its successors, and dedicated programs using other strategies, are showing how intelligent software, exploiting the features of the newly-emerging AI languages, will be able to provide the problem-solving capability required in new-generation systems. There is still much development needed in this field to satisfy the defined fifth-generation performance criteria.

AUTOMATIC DEDUCTION, INFERENCE

As we have seen (with GPS), automatic deduction and theorem

---

* GPS was originally written in IPL-V which, like LISP, is a list-processing language useful for modelling psychological phenomena.

proving are closely related to problem-solving. The Logic Theorist is an automatic deduction system for propositions in logic. Wang (1960) has developed a reasonably efficient, complete algorithm for proving theorems in propositional logic, and efforts have been made to describe a logically-complete method for proving theorems in first-order predicate calculus. For example, the approach of Robinson (1965) is usually described in terms of *resolution* procedures (the resolution principle is exploited as the basic rule of inference), an approach that has had a major impact on commonsense reasoning and problem-solving.

Automatic deduction has usually been discussed in terms of classical first-order logic, a circumstance that is unhelpful to many commonsense concepts. For fifth-generation systems to embody, in part, a capacity for commonsense inference, it will be necessary to explore a range of 'higher-order' logics. It remains to be seen how relevant the work on classical logic will be to the new demands (see discussion in Cohen and Feigenbaum, 1982).

Various 'non-standard' logics have been highlighted recently, and these may be expected to influence fifth-generation approaches to the different modes of inference. Minsky (1980), for example, has written about *nonmonotonic* logic, noting that to treat commonsense reasoning as purely deductive is to ignore one of its crucial features – the ability to withdraw a conclusion in the light of new evidence. Work in this area (eg Bobrow, 1980) may be regarded as developing a sound theoretical basis for types of reasoning that do not follow a simple classical deductive approach. This may be seen as highly relevant to efforts to make fifth-generation systems more humanlike in their 'thinking' processes.

LEARNING

It will be useful, perhaps essential, for fifth-generation computers to have learning capabilities. At a mundane level, learning is a simple concept: simply to input new information into a system is analogous to a child learning 'by being told'. At a different level a system may be able to learn while carrying out a task, and to learn in such a way that future performances are carried out in an improved fashion. It emerges that there are many different ways to learn: some are embodied in current computer systems, and some will have to await the development of fifth-generation intelligence.

Boden (1977) observed that learning can be divided into various types: for instance, learning by example, learning by being told, and learning by doing (providing, respectively, 'new knowledge of cues and models, new knowledge of facts, and new skills'). Learning may consist of acquiring new data – a commonplace function in traditional computer systems – or it may be necessary to abandon old data superseded by new (more accurate or more up-to-date) information. The various knowledge bases in fifth generation will need to be able to grow and change in various ways. Learning programs are able to apply various strategies to affect a body of stored information.

Various programs have been developed to recognise physical objects in the environment (such a provision is closely linked to the various perceptual abilities; see Pattern Recognition, below). J. M. Tenenbaum has developed a program which has been taught to recognise the door, chairs, tables, pictures, etc, in grey-scale photographs of an office: the program may be shown a telephone, whereupon it learns to pick out telephones in the pictures. In this way, it can learn to identify a wide range of items by way of ostensive definitions.

In this approach, two data structures – semantic and image-storing (this latter termed 'iconic') – are employed to represent the concepts learnt. The semantic representation of a telephone, for instance, is developed in a discriminatory fashion in conjunction with an iconic representation of the same item. In the semantic network there are pointers to the iconic storage, so allowing the concepts to be defined pictorially even though they include abstract descriptions. The program can learn what something looks like, either by way of example or by being told that the item resembles something seen earlier. Boden (1977) describes in detail how the two data structures can be used to enable the program to learn to recognise, say, table-tops – given that it began with no knowledge of them.

This approach requires that the program can draw on a large body of knowledge – about surface orientations, colours, the nature of spaces, etc. The information must be accessed quickly, and specific descriptions must be translated into more general ones. These requirements suggest that learning in this way requires a cognitive system that can manipulate and analyse complex symbols. A program from P. H. Winston – able to recognise such structures as tables, arches, pedestals and arcades – illustrates this point. And research with primates, and with programs, has suggested that learning requires the storing of complex internal representations. (As far back as 1949, Harlow proposed the formation of 'learning sets' in monkeys, and there has been speculation that the traditional reinforcement methods used to establish learning in animals could be adopted in program design: when a system behaves in a certain 'approved' way, system changes could be caused which would increase the likelihood of similar behaviour being adopted in the future. This would allow a more impressive degree of learning than when a computer is simply fed with new information.)

There is a sense in which any inference-making capability allows the generation of new propositions and so allows facts to be accumulated which were not formerly stored in the system. For example, a program may draw certain conclusions on being told that 'such and such' is the case. The ability to draw such conclusions represents a type of learning, with the corollary that the degree of inferential skill in a system would, in part, define its learning competence.

Other programs learn by doing (ie they learn in the working situation). Colby's classic female-neurotic program, for instance, develops an idiosyncratic manner of coping with anxiety-ridden beliefs over a series of runs. During the early stages the program records which defence mechanisms are most effective in reducing 'emotional charges', and these become readily accessible for subsequent runs. A wide range of games programs also learn by doing: the celebrated Samuel draughts program remembers past successes to improve its current performance, using both 'rote learning' and 'learning by generalisation' to enable the program to benefit from experience. (The Samuel program regularly beat its creator, and in 1974 Donald Michie quoted a draughts champion who was beaten by the program: 'In the matter of the end game, I have not had such competition from any human being since 1954, when I lost my last game.')

Some programs can also learn from mistakes, as well as from successes. For example, STRIPS (the STanford Research Institute

Problem Solver) and HACKER (a term often applied to obsessive programmers) have been cited as programs that learn more intelligently than does the Samuel draughts-player.

STRIPS – used, for instance, to allow the SRI SHAKEY robot to perform in an intelligent way – can work out a means-ends analysis of a task and express a plan in terms of a sequence of necessary actions. The correct order for the actions is worked out, and an indication is given of which actions satisfy preconditions for other actions. Furthermore, an indication is provided of how SHAKEY's world – mostly seven rooms connected by eight doors and containing large boxes – changes progressively as the stipulated plan is implemented. The central reason for the plan is elucidated by the representation, and the plan has sufficient flexibility to allow it to be adapted to new circumstances. The program is equipped to learn from problem-solving experience, both by storing its worked-out decision (the plan) and by developing suitable generalisations.

G. J. Sussman's HACKER program can, in a similar way, learn general lessons from particular experiences, and so improve its performance with practice. When mistakes are made, following a trial-and-error attempt in a situation, the program tries to analyse what went wrong and why: if possible, the mistake is then generalised and added to a file of 'traps', to be avoided in future. The adjustment is generalised as a subroutine which can be used when necessary. The HACKER program occupies the simulated blocks world that is also inhabited by Winograd's SHRDLU (HACKER often has to *learn* procedural strategies that are already incorporated in SHRDLU).

It is obvious that the requirement that fifth-generation systems *learn* can be tackled in various ways. AI programs that facilitate learning according to a range of different strategies have drawn on what we know of learning in human beings and other animals. This type of development will clearly continue but computers may also evolve their own characteristic learning modes.

NATURAL LANGUAGE, UNDERSTANDING

To make fifth-generation computers accessible to the widest possible range of human users, it will be necessary for the systems to understand natural language. We will, for example, be able to speak to computers, and they will understand and answer back (see also Chapter 5). However, AI researchers have experienced great difficulty in writing programs that will enable computers to understand natural language. Even the simplest programs in this area are highly complex, and the most sophisticated programs still have limited scope, remaining confined to relatively narrow semantic domains. Early efforts at *machine translation* were largely unsuccessful since good translation depends upon effective understanding, a difficult concept to incorporate into programs.

Ideas on machine translation can be traced to the 1930s (to such workers as Smirnov-Troyansky in the Soviet Union and Artsouni in France), with the real work beginning in the immediate post-war years. Some of the developments in this field were based on the code-breaking successes of the war period. In 1947, A. D. Booth and D. H. V. Britten wrote a program for dictionary lookup (here each variant of a basic word – eg *love, loves, loving* – had to be stored as a separate entry), and in the following year R. H. Richens proposed rules for the inflections of words to eliminate the redundancy of multiple dictionary entries. In 1949, Warren Weaver distributed a memorandum *('Translation')* to about 200 specialists, stimulating much interest. Soon after, work began in several US research establishments, and a number of significant breakthroughs occurred. For example, A. G. Oettinger designed one of the first programs to carry out a word-to-word Russian-to-English translation. In 1954, a journal for mechanical translation (MT) was established.

The considerable difficulties in achieving satisfactory machine translation led to the pessimistic conclusion of the 1966 ALPAC report (made to the National Research Council after a year of study by its Automatic Language Processing Advisory Committee):

> 'Machine Translation' presumably means going by algorithm from machine-readable source text to useful target text, without recourse to human translation or editing. In this context, there has been no machine translation of general scientific text, and none is in prospect.

The report (influenced by the experiences of Bar-Hillel) discouraged funding in MT projects, though the early-1970s saw a revival of interest – partly because progress had been made in knowledge representation (ie the cognitive base for automatic language translation had broadened). Today there are various operational machine translation systems in the world. Lawson (1981) points out that there are about twenty such systems around the world, though these vary widely in competence.

In some cases it is useful to have even a bad translation, if this can be done quickly. Some systems may handle texts using a restricted form of the language, rendering translation easier. And other automatic facilities may focus on particular subtasks – such as dictionary lookup – or may, as with the bad translation, rely on a human editor to produce a final version of the text. It must be emphasised that good translation relies upon the machine (or the person) *understanding* the text, with understanding being recognised as a key concern of AI researchers in whatever area.

There are various approaches, apart from translation, to the question of how machines may be enabled to understand natural language. Klir and Valach (1965) proposed various definitions of 'understanding of text by machine':

— a machine understands a text if it gives correct answers to questions whose answering follows from the text;

— a machine understands a text if it gives correct answers to questions whose answering follows from the given text on the one hand, and from its prior store of knowledge on the other hand;

— the machine understands a text if it links up the knowledge resulting from it with its prior knowledge in the correct manner.

Finally, they generalise the definition of understanding in a way that avoids the excessive dependence upon a *verbally expressed relationship:* 'The machine understands the given signal (set of signals) if it adequately changes its former behaviour as a result of having received it'. Every signal has a certain significance for the machine, and newly-arriving signals are allowed to modify the machine's knowledge base.

It has been proposed that individuals move through a three-step process in recording information: first, a sentence is divided into *given* and *new* information; given information is located in memory; and new information is added to memory. This approach (eg Clark and Clark, 1977) was made explicit by Miller and Johnson-Laird (1976), examining perception and language, in developing the analogy with programming a computer. A computer first compiles a program written in a high-level language into the language that the machine can comprehend, and then the compiled program is performed using the appropriate data. A person's psychological processing of a sentence may involve a similar two-step sequence: the natural language input is first translated into appropriate mental instructions, then the decision is taken whether, say, to answer a question or to carry out a command; the second ('execution') phase involves searching memory and constructing a plan based on environmental data.

Language is important as a cognitive concern because of its direct connection with information *(knowledge* in an intelligent system). It is through language that communication (conversation) is possible, with criteria emerging for recognising understanding in human beings and computer systems. Partly for this reason, efforts have been made to develop conversational computer programs, one of the most celebrated being Joseph Weizenbaum's ELIZA (written in 1966 and named after the professor's pupil in Shaw's *Pygmalion*).

If ELIZA carries out any linguistic processing it does so at only a very primitive level. It relies on a system of fixed patterns of response that provide a superficial impression of language understanding. ELIZA is a 'psychiatric' program, able to provide an interview with a patient – by generating responses called up from a set of stored sentences. For example, if the program detects the word 'mother' in a statement made by the patient it responds with one of several stock sentences, such as 'Tell me more about your mother'. Weizenbaum himself acknowledged that ELIZA operated at a very superficial level, and he became concerned that people were taking ELIZA's 'conversational' ability* too seriously.

---

* Various observers have enjoyed comparing conversations of ELIZA with those of Arthur C Clarke's Hal in *2001: A Space Odyssey*.

Today it is widely acknowledged that there are weaknesses in the ELIZA system (for example, it cannot cope with compound sentences). However, as an early conversational facility, ELIZA was of landmark significance. Today, a version of the program is available for microcomputers (on 5¼-inch disks, for example, to run on an Apple II). And efforts have been made to reverse the roles: one classic Colby program, already mentioned, is a simulation – for conversational purposes – of a neurotic female patient.

Various 'understanding programs' have been developed in a way that relies upon specific conceptual features of the language. In the early-1970s, Roger C Schank of Yale University produced programs that were able to process natural language sentences about human actions. The programs rely on what Schank calls primitives of conceptual dependency, including MTRANS (actions in which information is transferred, such as telling and reading), ATRANS (where there is a transfer of possession, such as buying and giving), and ATTEND (actions involving sensing, such as watching and tasting). The programs can analyse the content of the discourse and also the meaning of the words. In some cases a syntax analyser can be used to determine the most likely parsing and interpretation of a sentence. Waltz (1982) has nicely illustrated the 'diagrams of conceptual dependency'.

Research is being applied to the generation of systems that allow human users to interrogate a database by means of natural language, and today at least one natural language system, Intellect, is in wide use outside research establishments. Intellect provides natural language access to information stored in its own memory. The system produces reports and replies in answer to queries such as:

Are there people working as secretaries and earning a salary of $15,000 or more?

What is the family status of the area managers that live in New York?

In one sense the system understands what it is being asked: it can be questioned in English and can give an English reply. In another sense, as with ELIZA, it is merely responding in a simple fashion to requests to access and correlate items of information. This facility adds little to our understanding of cognitive faculties in machines.

Marvin Minsky (of MIT) has suggested that all thinking, including language, might depend upon processes driven by expected structures of knowledge (termed 'frames'). Like Schank's primitives of conceptual dependency, a frame comprises a core and a set of slots, each slot corresponding to an aspect of a concept implicitly defined by the frame. The function of the frame is to represent a 'stereotype', an intuitively plausible model of the process file in information about a situation where the information is not explicitly mentioned. Various language-understanding programs now use this approach. Waltz cites a program written by Wendy Lehnert of Yale which can answer questions about stories; and a program (FRUMP) which can summarise news stories as they appear on the wire service of United Press International.

Efforts to build 'understanding programs' are limited by what is known about cognitive systems in human beings. If we do not know how a *person* uses cognitive facilities to understand metaphor, allusion, commonsense, etc, it is difficult to build such facilities into *machines*. It is for this reason that the reciprocal influence between cognitive psychology and artificial intelligence is so important in modern research.

Some artificial systems have impressive levels of understanding. For example, the robot kitchen worker, LUIGI, able to carry out a range of kitchen tasks and to answer questions about them, is provided with real-world descriptions of physical objects, a mental world of abstract concepts, and information about conceptual relations (Scraggs, 1975). It has been suggested that the LUIGI system could be extended to other environments. It is obvious that research into artificial understanding is proceeding on several fronts, and that fifth-generation requirements will encourage work in these various AI areas.

PATTERN RECOGNITION

Effective pattern recognition is essential to perception in human beings and other intelligent systems: it will be crucial to the intelligent man/machine interfaces in fifth-generation computers. It is necessary, not only to collect and store information, but also to interpret it, and in many cases this requirement can be seen as involving tasks in pattern recognition. Allport (1980) has declared that *'The basic mechanism of thought is seen as a process of pattern recognition'* (original italics).

In human beings, pattern recognition is a prodigious ability, whereas in computers it is rudimentary. Robots are gradually evolving sensory equipment but their perceptual facilities are primitive. Naomi Weisstein (1973) has indicated the difficulty that a computer faces in performing a relatively straightforward perceptual task: for example, to find a clock, perceive the time, and say what it is. Human beings have a rich body of contextual information to draw on, and we have evolved sophisticated search strategies. (We detect appropriate signals and convert these into a form the brain can understand: our eyes alone can transmit 4.3×10^6 bits of information to the brain per second.) The development of knowledge engineering for artificial systems may be expected to enlarge the cognitive framework in which a range of intelligent activities, including efficient pattern recognition, will be possible.

It is relatively easy for computer mechanisms to detect particular shapes (eg letters) when they are clear and well defined, and when they occupy expected positions. The recognition of 'feature combinations' can be achieved using sequential or parallel processing. In parallel processing, use is made of a 'pandemonium' model, where each individual feature is examined by an individual decision 'demon', each of which is able to respond to a specific input stimulus.

Various programs have been written to respond to complex shapes (such as triangles). For example, the 1968 Guzman program, called SEE, identifies points of conjunction of lines (vertices), which provide information about complex geometric objects. And various researchers have extended the program to recognise the structural features of geometric forms. Other programs recognise lines, regions, etc. Such techniques are aiding photographic enhancement and other useful tasks.

'Templates' are often used for the recognition of alphanumeric characters and other shapes, template-matching models relying upon matching the input to the shape's stored representation. Again, this approach works best when the shape is well defined and predictable in position (efforts involving preprocessing have been made to improve the pattern-matching competence of AI systems). Work has also focused on producing programs that will enable computers to recognise 'natural patterns' such as electrocardiograms, clouds, fingerprints and blood cells. (In 1982 it was announced that Logica was to provide a fingerprint storage and matching system for New Scotland Yard, London.)

Systems have been described (eg by Travis, 1982) that use the characteristics of associative memory to aid pattern recognition. Here related and concurrent pattern-generating signals are stored in such a way that the reoccurrence of one will cause the related signals to be generated. With this approach a signal can be regenerated using a new signal that is only similar, not identical, to an original. This capability is often used in real life where hazy or incomplete images have to be recognised. Travis has concluded that such a pattern-recognition facility could be used to improve man/machine communication, to take decisions, to aid data retrieval, to facilitate translation, etc. The system would have application to robotics: 'The ability to simultaneously correlate numerous inputs would enable a system to communicate easily with its controllers; to have a sense of position within an environment; to coordinate vision and movement; to maintain balance; etc, as well as performing tasks'.

There is growing recognition that it is possible to analyse *perception as a computational process* (see the chapter with that title in Sloman, 1978), and that prior knowledge is essential to efficient perceptual performance. Sloman has highlighted the various conscious and unconscious achievements that contribute to successful perception in human beings:

— discerning features in the sensory array;

— deciding which features to group into larger units;

— deciding which features to ignore;

— deciding to separate unrelated contiguous fragments;

— making inferences;

— correctly interpreting given data as something quite different;

— using inconsistencies to redirect attention or to reinterpret;

— recognising pointers to a particular interpretation.

An efficient pattern recognition or perceptual mechanism, whether natural or artificial, has to be capable of these and other, related, achievements.

The approach to computational pattern recognition is developing on several fronts, and not all the developments relate to visual phenomena. Speech recognition systems rely on recognising sound patterns (Chapter 5). For example, a voice recognition and synthesis system, called Automatic Answer Network System for Electrical Requests (Anser), has been developed by Nippon Telegraph and Telephone (NTT) to facilitate, via pattern recognition techniques, communication between banks and their customers. And language understanding programs use various pattern-matching facilities.

The SIR (Semantic Information Retrieval) program, written in LISP by Bertram Raphael in 1968, matches sentences against 24 matching patterns (such as: * is * and *how many * does * have?*). Similarly, Daniel Bobrow's STUDENT program recognises subsets of English derived from a set of basic patterns (such as: *what are * and *, *find * and **, and * is **). Weigenbaum's ELIZA (see above) has been represented as the most famous of the pattern-matching natural language programs.

Pattern recognition, whether concerned with visual or other types of phenomena, will be a key element in the development of user-friendly computer systems. As such, whether a part of natural language processing or real-world sensing, it will be increasingly important to fifth-generation computers. And again the point is highlighted: the various elements in AI and cognitive techniques constantly merge and overlap. We have seen that pattern recognition, natural language understanding and knowledge engineering are intimately connected: none of these areas is immune to developments in the others. It is obvious that the approach to intelligent new-generation systems is a multifaceted activity, and that the development of true fifth-generation computers will depend upon research successes in many different fields.

AUTOMATIC PROGRAMMING

Automatic programming, important to fifth-generation development, is represented as automation of some part of the programming process. Already, small programs have been generated from
a specification of what the program is intended to do. Barr and
Feigenbaum (1982) have declared that 'in a sense, all of AI is a
search for appropriate methods of automatic programming'.

The early development of compilers was a step towards automatic programming (in fact the first FORTRAN compiler was termed
an 'automatic programming' system). Today AI is seen as the
ability of programs to reason about what they actually do, which is
why LISP's ability to manipulate programs as data is important.
The ability to reason about programs is a central research goal of
automatic programming. The development of such facilities may
be regarded as saving people from programming chores, or as
generating programs that are beyond the scope of human programmers. Put another way, automatic programming will allow the
programmer to specify the task at a higher and more natural level –
and this is of particular significance to fifth generation. The more
'naturally' a problem can be represented to a computer for solution, the less the need for human programming expertise. As we
may expect, automatic programming is linked to natural language
understanding.

The various automatic-programming systems are characterised
by:

— *a specification method*. *Formal* specification methods may
   be very-high-level programming languages, and they may
   or may not be interactive. It is also possible to use *specification by examples* or to employ, often interactively, natural
   language;

— *a target language*. This is the language in which the system
   writes the finished program (typically, LISP, PL/1 and
   GPSS);

— *a problem area*. This relates to the intended application. For
   example, the NLPQ system is concerned with queueing
   problems, and Protosystem I is concerned with inventory

control and other tasks. The type of problem area can affect the method of specification;

— *a method of operation.* Existing automatic-programming systems use a variety of methods, including: theorem proving, program formation, knowledge engineering, automatic data selection, traditional problem-solving, and induction. The various approaches overlap, and a system may draw on features from several.

There are now many functioning automatic-programming systems (NLPQ, PSI, PECOS, DEDALUS, SAFE, LIBRA, etc) and the range is likely to further expand with developments in AI in general and such topics as knowledge engineering in particular. Progress in such systems will directly influence the intelligence and user-friendliness of fifth-generation computers.

Some automatic-programming systems have achieved remarkable results. For example, the ID3 system, developed by Ross Quinlan of the Basser Department of Computer Science at the University of Sydney, has taught itself to solve a chess problem, writing its own program of instructions 'which is about five times more efficient than the best program the computer's "master" could come up with' *(New Scientist,* 17/1/80).

In developing ID3, the computer was presented with different chess positions, and was told in each case that the game would, or would not, end in three moves. Key positional properties were identified and rules established for game termination. Then the rules were translated into LISP. The best LISP program written by Quinlan took 17.5 milliseconds to run successfully on a CDC Cyber machine in Sydney: the ID3-written program took 3.4 milliseconds.

It is this sort of impressive development that has urged Donald Michie to recommend the provision of a 'human window' in all computer systems – so that people will remain aware of what is going on. This applies to aspects of automatic programming as it does to other areas of artificial intelligence. It is significant that some systems are not only reaching unpredictable conclusions but are doing so in ways that are opaque to human understanding.

SUMMARY

This chapter has surveyed a range of AI topics that are relevant to fifth-generation development. Some of the topics – automatic deduction, problem-solving, understanding natural language – are in the mainstream of fifth-generation research: other AI topics – game-playing, poetry-writing, etc – may appear to be less relevant but may, in fact, yield research conclusions that aid the development of intelligence in artificial systems. Game-playing, for instance, can enlarge human knowledge of the broad heuristic techniques that are necessary in solving economic, social and other problems in conditions that are constantly changing and difficult to define.

An effort has also been made to point out that modern AI research is now part of cognitive science, that fifth-generation systems are likely to be affected by current research into the cognitive faculties of human beings and other animals. This type of consideration has always intrigued certain types of computer specialist, though efforts to model human psychological processes and to construct systems that mirror the flexible intelligence of living systems have generally been regarded as eccentric or fanciful. Today, for the first time, building on the early AI work, there is a serious effort – international and massively funded – to develop cognitive faculties for artefacts.

4 Expert Systems

INTRODUCTION

Expert systems are often regarded as representing a subclass of artificial intelligence, and they are often (wrongly) identified with fifth-generation computers. Expert systems have been working – with varying degrees of success – for many years, whereas we do not expect to see true fifth-generation configurations until around the end of the decade. However, as (usually) conversational systems relying on progress in knowledge engineering, expert systems are one of the key developments contributing to the fifth-generation programme.

In one view (eg Addis, 1982), the range of expert systems represents degrees of enhancement to an information retrieval system. This type of interpretation is obviously plausible: the competence of the human expert largely resides in fancy information retrieval skills, and whatever the ideal purpose of the artificial system it is easy to extend the analogy, in this context, between machine and human capability. It has been pointed out that much of human problem-solving is possible through the exploitation of 'non-standard' logics, allowing a flexibility that is not yet possible in artificial systems, but it is for this reason that the various facets of inference-making are being explored as part of fifth-generation research.

An expert system may be regarded as a means of recording and accessing human competence in a particular specialist field. The most robust interpretation (eg Duda et al, 1980) suggests that an expert system is capable of humanlike performance and can serve thereby as a replacement expert. Less ambitiously, expert systems may be seen as exhibiting competence in a relatively narrow agreed domain, serving as tools to aid communication between human experts. (It is hard to see this latter interpretation not progressively yielding to the former with advances in knowledge engineering and other areas.) The fact that no expert system has so far been built for completely naive human users underlines one particular thrust behind the fifth-generation research programme: here a central aim is to make computer capability, embodied in expert and other types of systems, available to the widest possible range of users. If current expert systems are reasonably seen to lack natural human performance features then fifth-generation systems will be less limited – and, ideally, they will be found in schools, offices, shops and the home, as well as in the specialist research environments which have tended to be the domain of working expert systems.

We have seen that work in information retrieval (IR) is likely to influence the development of expert systems. A main purpose of IR is to extract relevant information from a large store of data. The elements in the store are usually assigned index terms which the user specifies, in some combination, to obtain the required information. One key problem is that the index terms, in different concatenations, are capable of many different interpretations: when words are combined in phrases, there can be many subtle variations that are difficult to express in Boolean or other types of formal logic. This circumstance may make it difficult for the user to obtain the specific information that he requires. This type of problem is common to the development of both IR facilities and expert systems.

One approach to information retrieval is to develop a model of the stored data so that it is homomorphic with respect to user requests. Such a model would feature the index terms in defined relationships in order to aid information selection in the particular subject area. Again, work in this area has direct relevance to requirements in both mainstream IR and expert systems: Addis (1982), for example, has noted what he sees to be 'an evolutional convergence of what may seem to be two distinct sciences'.

Some of the most successful expert systems are now relatively well known and have been operating for several years. Typical of such systems are MYCIN and INTERNIST (for medical diagnosis), DENDRAL and SECS (for chemical analysis), and PROSPECTOR (for geological prospecting) (see Actual Expert Systems, below). GPS (the General Problem Solver briefly considered in Chapter 3) has also been regarded as one of the earliest expert systems. DENDRAL and SECS are said to have 'as much reasoning power in chemistry as most graduate students and some Ph.Ds in the subject' (Cole, 1981).

The expert system SIR and its successor QA3 are question-answering systems exploiting the techniques of formal logic. The LUNAR program can answer questions about moon rock samples by drawing on a massive database provided by NASA: here procedural semantics allows questions to be automatically converted into a program to be executed by a sophisticated retrieval facility.

An initial step in generating an expert system may be to persuade a human expert to sit at a computer terminal and to type in his or her expertise. This can be an immensely difficult task: it is one thing to be an expert, quite another to be able to articulate the expertise in coherent propositions that are useful to a computer. Developments in knowledge engineering may be expected to aid the expert in this context.

Once the expert knowledge has been fed into the computer it is likely to exist within a tree-like structure, with specific items of knowledge existing as axioms or rules which can be viewed as nodes within the tree. At the top of the tree is the system's 'goal hypothesis', a statement about the problem which also has probability and margin-of-error features. The expert system may have one major goal hypothesis and a number of subsidiary goals, each goal being a statement about a circumstance of the situation. Many goal hypotheses, the low-probability contingencies, will not be included: in these circumstances the system will advise the user accordingly (eg 'Ask a *real* expert!').

The intelligence of the expert system may be evaluated, perhaps frivolously, by a version of the Turing test, one of the earliest conversational scenarios. (Here an operator is provided with a pair of terminals, one of which is connected to a human-controlled terminal while the other is connected to the artificial intelligence.

If, by asking questions and receiving answers, the operator cannot distinguish between human and machine then the machine is deemed to be intelligent.) A Turing test for expert systems would have one terminal operated by the expert and one operated by the expert system: if the operator could not tell the difference, then the artificial system would be deemed truly *expert*.

Most of the operating expert systems are in the US, but as with computers in general they will become commonplace in all the advanced countries of the world. The early-1980s saw the UK's first dedicated expert systems division set up at Racal Decca, aimed specifically at the oil industry. Systems Programming Ltd has developed the rule-based technique, pioneered by Donald Michie and others at Edinburgh, to produce the Sage package announced in May 1982. Now a dozen or so Sage systems have been delivered or ordered. ICL, for example, is using Sage for projects associated with the introduction of its DM/I and Estriel mainframe computers in 1984/5. Also, a political risk system has been developed for Shell as a demonstration of Sage's capacity. ICI and BHRA Fluid Engineering are using Sage systems to experiment with expert systems development: ICI is using the facility to aid development of a design and consultancy aid to examine pipe stress corrosion cracking, and BHRA is developing a system to gauge flow rates and patterns inside pipes by drawing inferences from data received from sensors. SPL is also developing an open-ended question-answering system.

Expert systems, a subclass of AI, are being developed for a variety of practical purposes. Expertise is collected from human beings and fed into systems with a capacity to store and manipulate the knowledge in response to subsequent user enquiries. When expert systems become truly user friendly, available to computer-naive operators, they will represent a key contributing element in the movement towards fifth-generation computers.

FEATURES OF EXPERT SYSTEMS

General

Expert systems are being developed to solve a range of practical problems. As with fifth-generation computers they represent a departure from, in particular, traditional methods of programming. Expert systems have been defined as (quoted by d'Agapeyeff, 1982):

> 'problem-solving programs that solve substantial problems generally conceded as being difficult and requiring expertise. They are called *knowledge-based* because their performance depends critically on the use of facts and heuristics used by experts'.

The body of facts (knowledge) and the heuristics (which may be regarded as 'rules of thumb') are represented in the computer. The program uses the heuristics to operate on the stored knowledge in the light of a user enquiry, and ideally the system's reasoning can be explained to the user to indicate how a particular conclusion was reached. The British Computer Society's Committee of the Specialist Group on Expert Systems has defined an expert system as:

> 'the embodiment within a computer of a knowledge-based component from an expert skill in such a form that the machine can offer intelligent advice or take an intelligent decision about a processing function. A desirable additional characteristic, which many would regard as fundamental, is the capability of the system on demand to justify its own line of reasoning in a manner directly intelligible to the enquirer. The style adopted to attain these characteristics is rule-based programming'.

This definition emphasises rule-based programming (ie programming in logic or relational languages, such as PROLOG), allows for a wide range of applications (ie not only to consultancy functions but also to data processing and on-line control systems), and indicates the desirability of an 'explanation-of-reasoning' capability (though this does not feature in many existing expert systems). Prototype expert systems already exist in such fields as medicine, engineering and molecular genetics, and Donald Michie has mentioned a business system designed to give advice on how to reduce income tax liability.

Expert systems represent a flexible approach to computer competence, drawing on specialist knowledge and exploiting various types of inference (not only deductive reasoning). Research and development in this area may be expected to complement the progress in the mainstream fifth-generation programme.

System Structure

Any expert system is characterised by three fundamental elements: the Knowledge Manager, the Knowledge Base and the Situation Model. These are shown in Figure 4.1 which includes a listing of alternative names found in the literature (following d'Agapeyeff, 1983).

The Knowledge Manager typically uses the information contained in the Knowledge Base to interpret the current contextual data in the Situation Model. Everything which is application-dependent can be kept in the Knowledge Base, allowing the Knowledge Manager to function as a multi-application tool. MYCIN, for example, advises on the diagnosis and treatment of bacterial infections (see Actual Expert Systems, below), and EMYCIN (or empty MYCIN) has been developed from the original system: a different Knowledge Base is used for different applications.

The more comprehensive the Knowledge Base, the less the strain upon the inferential logic inside the Knowledge Manager when a question has to be answered. This means that the power of the system tends to be defined according to its depth of knowledge rather than its ability to reason. In the event, however, the user will

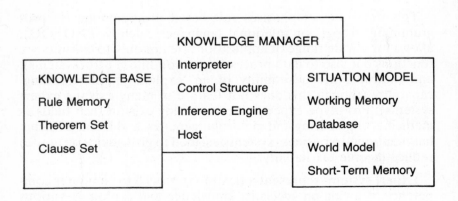

Figure 4.1   Main Elements in Expert Systems

only be interested in receiving a useful response to the initial query. It may be expected that an expert system will develop – as it accumulates more expertise, either directly as new information is fed in, or indirectly as the system remembers the results of useful inferences. In addition to operating on the Knowledge Base, the Knowledge Manager will also be concerned with knowledge acquisition (ie developing the Knowledge Base), knowledge updating (ie modifying the Knowledge Base), and providing explanations (ie explaining system features or details of operations such as inference-making). An expert system can operate at several levels – relatively superficially if a quick answer is sufficient, or more deeply if a more complex analysis is required.

Software

It may be emphasised that expert systems are largely about software. (This goes nicely with Margaret Boden's 'tin-can' view of computer hardware.) Expert systems have been written in traditional languages but there is much current focus on the use of PROLOG which has also been selected, as we have seen, as the fifth-generation 'kernel' language. Languages such as PROLOG are not concerned with handling numerical quantities but with expressing relationships. This makes them highly suitable for the inference mechanisms required in both expert systems and fifth-generation computers.

The use of *rules* (eg an *if then* relationship, see Knowledge Representations, below) can serve the development of a knowledge base built up in PROLOG. In this context, no distinction is drawn between a piece of factual information (eg an item of data) and a statement rule (eg a piece of program). Both can be held in the PROLOG database and can be selected when required. PROLOG statements may be seen as constituting both the specification of the program and the program itself.

Conventional high-level languages (eg FORTRAN and COBOL) are rich in syntax but weak in semantics. This is because the languages were intended for use by professional programmers engaged in different tasks in different companies, while semantics tends to be application-specific. By contrast, expert systems are necessarily rich in semantics, and independent of machines and architectures (though particular languages are suitable for, for example, data flow architectures).

Knowledge Representation, Rules

The various operating expert systems depend upon accumulating knowledge in the form of *rules*. One advantage of this approach is that the knowledge concerning the particular specialist area can be expanded incrementally; furthermore, it is in a form easily expressible by an expert. For example, the TEIRESIAS program, associated with MYCIN, collects rules from the expert, checks for rule consistency, and follows chains of reasoning to expose inadequate or inappropriate rules. A set of *meta-rules* is used to accumulate the diagnostic rules for MYCIN. The collecting of rules can be a time-consuming task.

The rules comprising the knowledge base are equivalent to an application program, and they may have many different formats; the *if*-a-condition-*then*-an-action format is very common, with the *then* section able to represent inferences, assertions, probabilities, precepts, etc. The first of several conditions associated with the rule determines whether the rule is potentially valid with respect to the current state of the situation model. A rule can require that a number of conditions be satisfied before an action is authorised. The following rule, for example, is from VM (Fagan, 1980), a system for monitoring the post-surgical progress of a patient requiring mechanical breathing assistance:

> *If* the current context is 'ASSIST"
> > *and* the respiration rate has been stable for 20 minutes
> > *and* the I/E ratio has been stable for 20 minutes
> *then* the patient is on 'CMV' (controlled mandatory
> ventilation)

In this case, involving a transition from 'ASSIST' to 'CMV', the first condition is a state value of, and the other two measurements in, the situation model. When the rule is triggered, the context state is changed: further rules subsequently update the situation model.

A typical rule from MYCIN –

> *If* the infection is primary-bacteremia

> *and* the site of the culture is one of the sterile sites
> *and* the suspected portal of entry is the gastro-intestinal tract
> *then* there is suggestive evidence (0.7) that the identity of the organism is bacteriodes –

shows how a conclusion can be assigned a probability rating: in this case there is a 7 out of 10 chance that the conclusion is true. This follows human practice closely, where much knowledge is inexact and partial (see Uncertainties, below).

Rules, as observed, define the knowledge in the system, with meta-rules used to manipulate rules. Some systems also have meta-meta-rules; rules at the various higher levels being analogous to system software in traditional configurations. Rule-based expert systems are now relatively common (see Actual Expert Systems, below), and it has been found that good performance can be achieved in various specialist areas using 200 to 300 rules. A number of rule-independent system languages (Rita, Rosie, Age, Hearsay III) are being developed, mostly in California.

There are three broad types of system organisations for rule systems. These (following Bond, 1981) are:

— *top-down*. Here, as in MYCIN, the system sequences through top-level goals or conclusions to see if any are true. An effort is made to match the right-hand side of rules to the goal. Where a match occurs, components on the left are set up as further goals, and so on, generating a goal tree. The system pursues each goal in turn, requesting, in the case of MYCIN, clinical information as it needs it;

— *model-based*. Unlike MYCIN, this type of system organisation relies upon a model of the relevant world. Rules use input data to establish and correct the model, and in particular the rules chart the time development of the model. This allows predictions to be made, and the past causation to be traced. In CASNET, for example, a model of the patient's condition is built up and maintained throughout the period of treatment. Features of multiple causation can be analysed and the patient's progress can be monitored and analysed;

— *blackboard*. Here the rules are organised into *knowledge sources* carrying expertise in particular areas. The knowledge sources operate, without communicating with each other, on a communal database (blackboard). The database contains hypotheses with certainty factors, and is organised to correspond to levels of data analysis. Hypotheses can be established or modified by the knowledge sources. The Hearsay speech understanding system is organised on this basis.

In addition, various other system organisations can be employed for rule manipulation. These possibilities relate directly to the four major areas being investigated in the context of knowledge representation: techniques for modelling and representing knowledge; methods enabling computers to think in natural language (since theories of inference and memory often rely on understanding how meaning is mapped onto the structure of language); techniques for deduction, problem-solving, commonsense reasoning, etc; and strategies for heuristic activity (eg allowing rapid focus on a small number of likely solutions among many possible ones). Knowledge representation and rule-based strategies are converging to enhance the competence of both the family of expert systems and the emerging fifth-generation computers.

A variety of knowledge representation techniques have already been exploited in AI programs that play games (such as chess and bridge), converse in natural language, operate robots, etc. For example, an early representation formalism was the *state-space representation,* used in game-playing and problem-solving. The structure of a problem is represented in terms of the alternatives available at each possible problem state. From any given state, all possible next states can be determined by means of *transition operators* (or *legal-move generators* in game-playing programs). One aim is to limit the number of alternatives to the best possibilities, an approach that requires programs that can reason using comprehensive knowledge about the relevant world. The overall goal is to deepen the AI programs' understanding of the problems which they are trying to solve.

Formal logic may be regarded as the classical means of representing knowledge about the world. Its progressive systematisation – from Aristotle, through de Morgan and Boole, to Frege and

Russell, and then to the modern logicians – has influenced directly computer science, artificial intelligence and, in particular, the inference mechanisms being developed for expert systems and fifth-generation computers.

In logic and the related formal systems, deductions can be guaranteed to be correct. The conclusions (the semantic entailment) that can be drawn from a set of logic statements are defined precisely by the laws of inference. This means, in principle, that a database can be kept logically consistent, and the derivation of new facts from old can be automated (though with a large number of facts, there tends to be an unmanageable combinatorial explosion of possibilities). In this approach, as elsewhere, there is need for more knowledge about relevance (eg ways of defining what facts are relevant to what situations).

The *procedural representation* of knowledge appeared in efforts to encode some explicit control of theorem-proving within a logic-based system. Knowledge about the world is contained in *procedures,* programs that know how to do particular things in well-defined situations. Here the underlying knowledge is not stated explicitly and cannot be extracted in a form that is easy for human operators to understand. Such an approach has been influential in AI research but has a number of disadvantages.

Other topics bearing on knowledge representation are *semantic nets* (invented as psychological models of human associative memory), *production systems* (developed as models of human cognition), and various special-purpose techniques. One new representation scheme is the *frame,* a data structure that is intended to include declarative and procedural information in predefined internal relations. There is much discussion about the ability of a frame to determine whether it is applicable in a given situation. (The various knowledge representation schemes are discussed in detail in Barr and Feigenbaum, 1982.)

Uncertainties

Much in human problem-solving and inference is uncertain, inexact and partial (ie *fuzzy*). In many circumstances where decisions have to be made, the facts are far from precise. However, traditional logics and traditional programming have relied upon tightly-defined categories, and upon full delineations of the elements that appear in a calculation or a process. Today expert systems need a more flexible approach, and this will become increasingly important in the progress towards fifth-generation computers.

The essence of a method that can be adapted for handling inexact facts within a computer program can be found in *fuzzy set theory* (Zadeh, 1965). A 'model of inexact reasoning', developed in MYCIN, uses equations that perform equivalent functions to expressions belonging to fuzzy sets. Here the membership values are regarded as certainty factors which are assigned constraints. The shape of an object, for example, might be described as 'rectangular (0.6), oval (0.2) and square (0.0)', where the numbers, ranging between the binary poles of 0 and 1, indicate a degree of certainty for each quality. In contrast to what occurs in a normal database, a feature can be multivalued and indecisive.

We are all acquainted with the linguistic devices in natural language that allow subtle distinctions to be made between the features of objects. Thus we can say that a colour is 'green*ish*' or '*sort of* orange-red'. This latter may be represented in a computer program as (Colour (Red 0.7) (Orange 0.3)) or as (Colour 6000), where 6000 denotes the wavelength of the light. Shaket (1976) has described a technique able to convert physical values to certainty (membership) values. These can then be modified by linguistic devices (eg 'very' 'rather', 'sort of', etc) to cause a shift in fuzzy set values in line with what a human being might expect.

The use of fuzzy set theory and related techniques in computer programs may be regarded as one of several means of developing machine competence (in, for example, expert systems and fifth-generation computers) to approach that of human beings. We have seen that efforts to make computer intelligence more 'humanlike' are a central element in the fifth-generation program.

Range of Applications

There are many applications, potential and actual, for expert systems. Webster (1983) reports that the UK Department of Health and Social Security is planning to use expert systems in its social security offices: people will be able to ascertain their entitlements and how to obtain payments. In another field, the introduction of the Isolink telecommunications software modules have brought expert systems as part of office automation a step nearer. The modules allow non-technical users of the Xibus multifunction workstation – without any knowledge of protocols, addresses, procedures, etc – to access computer systems, databanks, and network services.

Most working expert systems are employed in scientific or experimental use, but today there is a clear shift towards the commercial environment (we have already cited some commercial products) and towards practical applications in such areas as education and medicine (see Actual Expert Systems, below). And many expert systems are in development: for instance, in such areas as equipment failure diagnosis, speech and image understanding, mineral exploration, military threat assessment, advising about computer system use, VLSI design, and air traffic control. Expert systems will have a role to play whenever problems have to be solved or expert advice is needed.

MICROS, EXPERT SYSTEMS

No-one doubts that small computer systems will proliferate throughout the world in the years to come. In 1982, represented as a 'banner year' for small systems, no less than 1,440,000 such devices were sold worldwide, with more than one million sold in the US alone (a 70 per cent leap over 1981 sales). One prediction (in the journal *Byte,* January 1983) suggests that in the year 1991 around eleven million personal computers will be sold throughout the world. Colin Crook, managing director of Zynar, has suggested that by that time there will be 200 to 400 million personal computers in the world – and many of them will be powerful machines, programmed in PROLOG, and able to run hosts of expert systems.

Personal computers, a central element in the Japanese fifth-generation programme, will be parallel processing machines, individually based on as many as 32 processors, carrying 10 megabytes of memory, and working at a rate of 10 million instructions per second. It has been suggested (eg by Philip Hughes, chairman of Logica and a member of the Alvey group, see Chapter 6) that smart applications for personal computers may be the best way for the UK to exploit developments towards fifth-generation systems. Clive Sinclair has already hinted at the possibility of offering expert system packages for the Spectrum and later on for the ZX83 home system (this latter based on the ICL-Sinclair workstation, scheduled for launch in 1983). Logic Programming Associates has sold more than 100 copies of a MicroProlog compiler. It may be expected that the expert systems that will be of most use to personal computer users will be in the areas of problem-solving, question-answering and education.

At the same time the difficulty of putting really useful expert systems onto microcomputers should be noted. The PROSPECTOR expert system (see below), for example, written in a dialect of LISP called INTERLISP, has program listings running to more than 300 pages of source code. This requires a DEC mainframe to run. Faced with this weight of software, 'most micros would curl up and die' (Webster, 1983).

It is likely that expert system versions will soon be developed for microcomputers (much as a rudimentary ELIZA is available for an Apple II), but without the high-level competence of the fully-fledged systems. A version of PROLOG is being developed for the Sinclair Spectrum, and parallel developments will encourage the emergence of micro-based expert systems.

ACTUAL EXPERT SYSTEMS

General

A number of operating expert systems (MYCIN, PROSPECTOR, etc) have already been mentioned, but it is worth considering some of these – and related systems – in more detail. The systems outlined below exemplify a development that will become increasingly significant in the trend towards fifth-generation computers.

Medicine

Computers have been used for medical decision-making for about twenty years, employing programs that carried out well-established statistical procedures. In the main, the programs focused on the diagnostic element in consultation. Once symptoms had been presented, the computer would select one disease from a fixed set, using methods such as pattern recognition through discriminant functions, Bayesian decision theory, and decision-tree techniques. In more complex programs, *sequential* diagnosis was carried out. This involved specifying a new test for the patient in order to supplement insufficient information for a reliable diagnosis. Here the best test is selected according to economic factors, possible danger to the patient, and the amount of useful information that the test would yield.

By 1980 a wide range of diagnostic systems had been investigated. In one survey (Rogers et al, 1979), a table of 58 empirically tested computer-aided medical systems is presented (see Table 6).

In this context, computers are seen as having several inherent capabilities well suited to medical problem-solving:

— the ability to store large quantities of data, without distortion, over long periods of time;

Disease Type	Number of Studies
Endocrine, nutritional and metabolic	13
Blood and bloodforming organs	2
Mental disorders	10
Nervous system and sense organs	1
Circulatory system	5
Respiratory system	2
Digestive system	12
Genitourinary system	2
Pregnancy, childbirth and the puerperium	1
Skin and subcutaneous tissue	3
Musculoskeletal system, connective tissue	1
Symptoms, ill-defined conditions	4
Accidents, poisonings, violence	2
	Total 58

Table 6   Number of Articles in Computer-Aided Diagnosis
(See bibliography in Rogers et al, 1979)

— the ability to recall data exactly as stored;

— the ability to perform complex logical and mathematical operations at high speed;

— the ability to display many diagnostic possibilities in an orderly fashion.

Computer-based diagnostic systems can incorporate features to offset limitations in human diagnostic problem-solvers. For example, the short-term character of human memory can be a major limitation on effective problem-solving; and man has often been represented as a reluctant decision-maker, '. . . beset by conflict, doubts and worry, struggling with incongruous longings, antipathies, and loyalties . . .' (Janis and Mann, *Decision-Making,* Free Press, 1977).

The accuracy of a computer-based diagnostic system depends upon many factors: the depth of the data (knowledge) base, the complexity of the diagnostic task, the selected algorithm, etc. In the Rogers et al (1979) review of applications, it was found that 60 per cent of all the diagnostic studies used an algorithm based on Bayes' theorem. Furthermore, there was a correlation between the disease class and the kind of algorithm used to make the diagnosis. Some computer-based diagnostic systems have performed better than medical consultants, and it is likely that automatic diagnostic systems will be increasingly common in various medical areas. At the same time it is important to recognise the limitations of computer-based medical systems. Moreover, attention will have to be given to the psychological elements in using a computer in the consulting room (see, for example, Fitter and Cruickshank, 1982).

During the 1970s, efforts were made to apply AI techniques to problems in medical diagnosis. Again difficulties relating to inexact knowledge were evident: for instance, a particular treatment could not be guaranteed to result in a particular patient state. This situation stimulated the search for methods of representing *inexact knowledge* and for performing *plausible reasoning* (see Uncertainties, above). Diagnosis in the medical domain has been depicted as a problem of hypothesis formation, with clinical findings being used to generate a consistent set of disease hypotheses. The various expert systems devoted to medical diagnosis exploit different approaches to the task of hypothesis formation.

There are now many operating expert systems in medicine. Barr and Feigenbaum (1982) highlight typical programs (and also provide full bibliographic citations in each instance).

Attention has been drawn to MYCIN, CASNET, INTERNIST, PIP, the Digitalis Therapy Advisor, IRIS and EXPERT. In addition, there are various experimental programs being developed, including:

— PUFF, a pulmonary-function program;

— HODGKINS, a system for performing diagnostic planning for Hodgkins disease;

— HEADMED, a psychopharmacology advisor;

— VM, an intensive care monitor;

— ONCOCIN, a program for monitoring the treatment of oncology out-patients on experimental treatment regimens.

The MYCIN expert system is intended to provide consultative advice on diagnosis and treatment for infectious diseases. This is a useful facility because the attending physician may not be an expert on infectious diseases: for example, an infection may develop after heart surgery, with a consequent need for prompt treatment in conditions of uncertainty. We have already seen that medical knowledge is stored in MYCIN as a set of rules augmented by certainty factors. The factors are used to express the strength of belief in the conclusion of a rule, assuming that all the premises are true.

The MYCIN rules are stored in LISP form and individually comprise a piece of domain-specific information including an ACTION (often a conclusion) that is justified when the conditions in the PREMISE are fulfilled. Figure 4.2 shows a typical MYCIN rule (this is the LISP form of the rule given in English under Knowledge Representation, above).

Formal evaluations of MYCIN suggest that the system performance compares favourably with that of human experts on such diseases as bacteremia and meningitis. The TEIRESIAS system operates to allow the expert to inspect faulty reasoning chains and to augment and repair MYCIN's medical knowledge. There is a consensus that the MYCIN system shows great promise.

The Causal ASsociational NETwork (CASNET) program was developed at Rutgers University to perform medical diagnosis, with the major application in the field of glaucoma. Here the disease is not represented as a static state but as a dynamic process that can be modelled as a network of causally connected pathophysiological states. The system identifies a discerned pattern of causal pathways with a disease category, whereupon appropriate treatments can be specified. The use of a causal model also facilitates prediction of the development of the disease in a range of treatment circumstances.

CASNET, adopting a strictly bottom-up approach, works from tests, through the causal pathways, to final diagnosis. Though principally applied to glaucoma, the system exhibits a representational scheme and decision-making procedures that are applicable to other diseases. Ophthalmologists have evaluated CASNET and deemed it close to expert level.

The INTERNIST consultation program, developed at the University of Pittsburgh, operates in the domain of internal medicine. A list of disease manifestations (eg symptoms, laboratory data, history, etc) is presented to the system, and diseases that would account for the manifestations are diagnosed. The program then discriminates between competing disease hypotheses. Diagnosis in the field of internal medicine can be difficult because more than one disease may be present in the same patient.

PREMISE: (AND (SAME CNTXT INFECT PRIMARY-
                     BACTEREMIA)
                     (MEMBF CNTXT SITE STERILESITES)
                     (SAME CNTXT PORTAL GI)   )
ACTION   (CONCLUDE CNTXT IDENT BACTERIODES TALLY .7)

Figure 4.2   MYCIN Rule 050

The system's knowledge of diseases is organised in a disease tree, with use made of the *'form-of'* relation (eg hepatocellular disease is a form of liver disease). The top-level classification is by organs – heart disease, lung disease, etc. A list of manifestations, entered at the beginning of a consultation, evokes one or more nodes in the tree (when a model is generated for each evoked node). In this case, a diagnosis corresponds to the set of evoked nodes that account for all the symptoms. INTERNIST-I has been enhanced to form INTERNIST-II (which diagnoses diseases by dividing the disease tree into smaller and smaller subtrees). The system already carries more than 500 of the diseases of internal medicine, ie it is about 75 per cent complete, and practical clinical use is anticipated.

The Present Illness Program (PIP), being developed at MIT, focuses on kidney disease. The system's medical knowledge is represented in frames which centre around diseases, clinical states, and the physiological state of the patient: thirty-six such frames have been constructed to deal with kidney disease. Like INTER-NIST but unlike MYCIN, PIP is designed to simulate the clinical reasoning of physicians.

Other work at MIT, carried out by the Clinical Decision Making Research Group, has been concerned with developing programs to advise physicians on the use of the drug *digitalis*. It is assumed that a patient requires digitalis: the programs determine an appropriate treatment regimen and its subsequent management in these circumstances. This approach is unusual in that it focuses on the problem of continuing patient management. This system, the Digitalis Therapy Advisor, was evaluated by comparing its recommendations to the actual treatments prescribed by human consultants for nineteen patients. On average a panel of experts preferred the recommendations of the physician, but the program's recommendations were reckoned to be the same or better in 60 to 70 per cent of all the cases that were examined.

Another medical system, IRIS, was developed for building, and experimenting with, other consultation systems. The system, designed at Rutgers University and written in INTERLISP, is intended to allow easy experimentation with alternative representations of medical knowledge, clinical strategies, etc. It has assisted in the development of a consultation system for glaucoma.

The EXPERT (expert) system, again developed at Rutgers, is aimed at helping researchers to design and test consultation models. Its development has been influenced by work in building consultation models in such medical areas as rheumatology, ophthalmology and endocrinology. (Experimental models have been developed in other areas, eg chemistry, oil-well log analysis, laboratory-instrument use, and car servicing.)

What we are seeing is a proliferation of expert system programs devoted to (first-order) diagnosis and related tasks, and to the (second-order) development of consultation systems. Whatever the task of a medical expert, it should in principle be amenable to investigation (and subsequent simulation) using expert system methods.

Chemistry

Expert systems are now finding applications in many areas of scientific research and investigation: for example, in chemical analysis, geological prospecting, and the solution of mathematical problems in engineering and physics. Computer programs have been widely applied in all the sciences for many years, but specifically AI methods have had a more limited application. In, for example, non-numeric chemical reasoning problems, these methods have been applied to:

— identifying molecular structures in unknown organic compounds;

— planning a sequence of reactions to synthesise organic chemical compounds.

The identification of molecular structures is important to a wide range of problems in chemistry, biology and medicine. In many cases, the sophisticated analytic methods of x-ray crystallography may not be practical, and researchers must interpret data obtained in other ways, eg via mass spectrometry. Some tests allow the chemist to discover *molecular fragments,* subparts of the molecule, from which characteristic *constraints* can be derived. These constraints are interpreted as graph features in the representation of the molecule. Some of the current AI programs use similar data to generate small subsets of the theoretically-possible structures. The identification of molecular structures, using this type of approach, is being tackled by such expert systems as DENDRAL, CON-GEN, Meta-DENDRAL, and CRYSALIS. By contrast, such expert systems as LHASA, SECS and SYNCHEM are concerned with finding techniques for the laboratory synthesis of known substances.

The (Heuristic) DENDRAL program, following the formulation of the DENDRAL algorithm in 1964, identifies the possible molecular structures of constituent atoms that could account for the given spectroscopic analysis of the molecule under investigation. One main purpose of the heuristic approach was to replace the exhaustive method of the algorithm by a more economical strategy. The program achieved the objective by supplementing the DENDRAL algorithm with rules derived from expert chemists using mass spectrographic data. However, the chemists had difficulty in explicating their expertise, and the Meta-DENDRAL project was launched in 1970 to develop a means of inferring the rules of mass spectrometry from examples of molecular structures that had already been successfully analysed by human experts.

By the mid-1970s it was found that limitations on the DENDRAL algorithm allowed Heuristic DENDRAL to generate only acyclic structures (ie ketones, alcohols, ethers, amines, etc). In 1976 the CONGEN program was designed to function without the acyclic limitation.

The Heuristic DENDRAL project – from its late-1960s inception to the present – has yielded various significant results. Though the system knows far less than a human expert, it elucidates structures efficiently by searching through possibilities. Published papers (cited in Barr and Feigenbaum, 1982) have variously shown that the program can solve structure elucidation problems for complex organic molecules, and that – for example, in the analysis of mass spectra of mixtures of oestrogenic steroids – the program can perform better than human experts. DENDRAL programs have been employed to determine the structures of various types of molecules (eg terpeniod natural products, marine sterols, chemical impurities, antibiotics, insect pheromones, etc). CONGEN, deriving from the DENDRAL project, is in practical use by chemists to solve various types of problems in the elucidation of molecular structures.

Meta-DENDRAL, designed to infer the rules of mass spectrometry from known structures, learns by scanning hundreds of molecular structure/spectral data-point pairs and by searching the space of fragmentation rules for likely explanations. The rule set can be extended to accommodate new data. The proficiency of Meta-DENDRAL can be estimated in part by the ability of a DENDRAL program using derived rules to predict spectra of new molecules. In fact the program has rediscovered known rules of mass spectrometry for two classes of molecules; and, more importantly, it has discovered *new* rules for three closely-related families of structures (the mono-, di-, and tri-keto androstanes).

The CRYSALIS expert system focuses on protein crystallography, aiming to integrate various sources of knowledge to match the crystallographer's performance in electron-density-map interpretation. (This would fill an important gap in the automation of protein crystallography.) The concept of an electron density map generally denotes some pictorial representation (eg a three-dimensional contour map) of electron density over a certain region. The skilled crystallographer can study such a map to discover features allowing him to infer atomic sites, molecular boundaries, the polymer backbone, etc. In due course a structural model can be built to conform to the electron density map. Automation of this task requires a computational system that could generate, display and test hypotheses.

In CRYSALIS the hypotheses are represented in a hierarchical data structure, with knowledge sources able to add, change and test hypothesis elements on a 'blackboard' (see Knowledge Representation, above). The system can at present only perform a portion of the total task of interpreting electron density maps. The knowledge base is relatively small, but this is expanding and a capability is envisaged for the complete interpretation of medium-quality medium-resolution electron density maps.

We have already mentioned the three major organic synthesis programs. LHASA (Logic and Heuristics Applied to Synthetic Analysis), maintained at Harvard, is the earliest. This system yielded SECS (Simulation and Evaluation of Chemical Synthesis), now being developed at the University of California. SECS extended the LHASA approach by more extensively exploiting stereochemical and other types of information. The third major program of this sort, SYNCHEM (SYNthetic CHEMistry), is being developed at the State University of New York.

The main item of knowledge in chemical synthesis is the chemical reaction. Here a rule describes a) a situation in which a molecular structure can be changed, and b) the change itself. The programs use knowledge of reactions to design a synthesis route from starting materials to target molecule. In summary:

— the LHASA knowledge base, a set of procedures, contains very sophisticated chemistry knowledge but is difficult to update;

— the SECS knowledge base, carrying about 400 separate transforms, allows new transforms to be added without the need for program changes;

— the SYNCHEM knowledge base includes a library of reactions and commercially-available starting compounds. Chemists can modify the knowledge base without reprogramming.

Computer-aided chemical synthesis is regarded as a potentially valuable new facility for chemists, whether engaged in research or industrial manufacturing. A key factor in expert systems devoted to organic synthesis is how much they know about chemical reactions. The three main synthesis programs have all demonstrated their ability to find synthetic routes for organic materials.

Mathematics

MACSYMA, originally designed in 1968, is a large computer system used to assist mathematicians, scientists and engineers in tackling mathematical problems. It accepts symbolic inputs and yields symbolic outputs, and, in addition to its algebraic-manipulation competence, it includes a large numerical subroutine library. Today MACSYMA, running on a DEC KL-10 at MIT and accessed through the ARPA Network, is used by hundreds of US researchers. Many workers from government laboratories, universities and private companies spend much of every day logged in to the system.

As with many other expert systems, the performance of MAC-SYMA relies upon an extensive knowledge base. This enables the interactive system to perform more than 600 different types of mathematical operations, including differentiation, integration, equation solving, matrix operations, and vector algebra. MAC-SYMA currently comprises about 230,000 words of compiled LISP code and a similar amount of code written in the special MACSYMA programming language.

Many of the system algorithms were known before the development of MACSYMA, while others evolved during the system research. AI helped to frame the environment in which MACSYMA was born, and various AI-related capabilities are currently being developed in the system (for example, a new representation for algebraic expressions and a knowledge-based 'apprentice').

Geology

Various computer-based systems are being developed to aid geologists engaged in exploration tasks. One of the best known of these systems is PROSPECTOR, being developed at SRI International to help geologists working on problems in hard-rock mineral exploration. (PROSPECTOR made news in 1982 when it was given the same field study data about a region in Washington State as that used by experts in a mining company. The system concluded that there were deposits of molybdenum over a wide area. The geologists disagreed but when exploratory drilling was undertaken PROSPECTOR was found to be right.)

The user provides PROSPECTOR with information about a region (eg data on rock types, minerals, alteration products, etc), whereupon the program matches the information against its models. Where necessary, PROSPECTOR asks the user for more information to enable a decision to be reached. The user can intervene at any stage to provide new data, change existing information or request an evaluation from the system. A sophisticated inference network is used to control PROSPECTOR's reasoning, with network nodes corresponding to various geological assertions (eg *There is alteration favourable for the potassic zone of a porphyry copper deposit*). Rules are employed to specify how the probability of one assertion affects the probability of another (these inference rules are analogous to the production rules used in MYCIN).

A geologist using PROSPECTOR prepares a model as an inference network. The current system contains five different models (developed in cooperation with five consulting geologists): Koroko-type massive sulphide, Mississippi-Valley type lead/zinc, type A porphyry copper, Komatiitic nickel sulphide, and roll-front sandstone uranium. These models are collectively represented by 541 assertions and 327 rules. Using the models and input data, the system is able to adjust the probability of hypotheses in changing circumstances.

The five models have only recently been developed to the point when useful geological evaluations could be made. And many further models are needed for extensive coverage of the full prospecting domain.

Education

Computer technology has been applied to education since the early-1960s, with applications in such areas as course-scheduling, test-grading, and the management of teaching aids. One aim of CAI (Computer-Aided Instruction) research has been to build instructional programs that incorporate course material in lessons that are optimised for each student. In the Intelligent CAI (ICAI) programs that began to emerge in the 1970s, course material was conveyed independently of teaching procedures – to enable problems and comments to be generated differently for each student. Today, AI is influencing the design of programs that are sensitive to the student's strengths and weaknesses, and to the preferred style of learning.

Early research on ICAI systems tended to concentrate on the representation of the subject matter. Attention may be drawn to such benchmark efforts as: SCHOLAR, a geography tutor; SOPHIE, an electronics troubleshooting tutor; and EXCHECK, a logic and set theory tutor. These systems have a high level of domain expertise, which allows them to be responsive over a wide spectrum of interactive problem-solving situations. Other expert educational programs are:

— WHY, which tutors students in the causes of rainfall, a complex geographical process that is a function of many variables. This system exploits 'socratic tutoring heuristics' and is able to identify and correct student misconceptions. WHY began as an extension of SCHOLAR;

— WEST, described as a program for 'guided discovery' learning. The system, deriving from a board game, assumes that a student *constructs* an understanding of a situation or a task, the notion of progressively corrected misconceptions being central to this assumption. The learning student interacts with a 'Coach';

— WUMPUS, which again uses game techniques to teach a mixture of logic, probability, decision theory and geometry. In one version, the coach is WUSOR-II, a system that involves the interaction of various specialist programs. Four basic modules are used: Expert, Psychologist, Student Model, and Tutor. The system is recognised to be a useful learning aid;

— GUIDON, a program for diagnostic problem-solving which uses the rules of the MYCIN consultation system. A student engages in a dialogue about a patient suspected of having an infection, and learns how to use clinical and laboratory data for diagnosis purposes. This system goes beyond responding to the student's last move (as in WEST and WUMPUS) and repetitive questioning and answering (as in SCHOLAR and WHY);

— BUGGY, designed to identify a student's basic arithmetic misconceptions. The system can provide an explanation of why a student is making an arithmetic mistake. Experience has indicated that forming a model of what is wrong can be more difficult than performing the task itself. BUGGY can be used to train teachers to diagnose errors in the way that students work.

The above programs are essentially *teaching* systems, and other programs are available to assist *learning by doing*. Emphasis may be given to effective 'learning environments' such as LISP-based LOGO (and its most celebrated application, turtle geometry), the message-passing SMALLTALK (and its extension, THING-LAB), and the DIRECTOR animation system. Here powerful programming-language features are used with sophisticated graphics facilities. AI has contributed to expert systems in the educational environment, as elsewhere.

SUMMARY

This chapter has highlighted some of the main features of expert systems, giving attention to such aspects as system structure, software, and knowledge representation. An indication has also been given of the relevance of AI to expert systems, and how expert system developments relate to the broad fifth-generation programme. Finally, some practical expert systems, operating in various fields, have been briefly profiled.

Expert systems, in common with other computer developments, are extending the power of artificial mechanisms in society. Their continued evolution depends, not only on the development of ever more sophisticated technologies, but also on new insights into human cognitive psychology.

5 Man/Machine Communications

INTRODUCTION

A central aim in the fifth-generation programme is to develop *user-friendly* computers, an important requirement if 'computer-naive' people are to be able to make full use of computer power. This means that users will be able to communicate with computers by means of natural language, and that this will be done aurally and in other ways. Already people are communicating with computers in various ways, and these methods often effect how people communicate with each other. Man/machine communication is possible by means of speech, touch, sight, handwriting, gestures, pictures, typing, printing, etc.

The use of keyboards has proved highly effective in allowing users to communicate with machines. When a key is pressed, there is no ambiguity about which character is indicated. The action can be translated into the required binary representation or into some intermediate form, such as punched card or magnetic tape, for subsequent input to the computer. But the use of a keyboard does not have the immediacy of spoken words, and moreover it usually implies knowledge of a high-level, or some other, computer language. Communication with a computer by means of speech would be preferable, particularly where this could be achieved using the natural language (English, French, Japanese, etc) of the user. Research into such possibilities is an important element in the fifth-generation programme.

In a paper presented at the 1981 fifth-generation computer conference (Tokyo), Hozumi Tanaka et al outline the approach to

139

be adopted to the man/machine interface. They begin by emphasising how human beings communicate with each other: a variety of forms of communication are used – 'natural language, both spoken and written, pictures, images, documents and the like'. Since computers are not usually equipped with *intelligent man/machine interfaces* they have difficulty in understanding these modes of communication. A main objective of fifth-generation research is to provide computers with this sort of intelligence.

INPUT/OUTPUT METHODS

One of the earliest methods of input to computers was by means of punched cards: using a keyboard, the operator translated the input into holes, set out in coded patterns, in the cards (paper tape was prepared in the same way). Then a card reader peripheral would scan the cards and feed the appropriate digital information into the computer. Later it became possible to convey the required information directly from the keyboard to magnetic media such as disks and (magnetic) tape, and directly to storage elements within the computer.

A key depression may indicate, not only a character or digit, but also a function (such as 'display the next page of information' or 'start the robot on its programmed task'). The keyboard may resemble a conventional QWERTY keyboard, though experiments are being carried out with different arrangements of keys; or there may be fewer or more keys. A small *keypad,* with relatively few keys, may be used for specific purposes, or a keyboard may carry a large number of keys to allow a wide range of data and functions to be input to the computer. The keyboard usually operates in conjunction with a display – to indicate what information and instructions have been keyed in, and to signal the computer's response when the system is working in *interactive mode.*

Experiments with new, more 'humanlike' methods of conveying information to a computer and receiving a response are characteristic of fifth-generation research. For example, speech may be regarded as a natural means of communication (see Voice Recognition and Speech Synthesis, below). Spoken words have characteristic sound patterns. *Voice recognition* systems are designed to recognise the patterns and, in more sophisticated systems, to *understand* what the words signify. After the information has been processed, a *speech synthesis* response may be initiated (the computer talks back to the user).

Typically, voice recognition systems have needed to be 'trained' by their human users: the systems, user-dependent, learn to recognise the voice of a particular person. Voice patterns are stored so that when particular words are spoken by the same person, the computer compares the patterns and selects the correct words. Such systems are limited to one user, cannot recognise continuous speech, and have small vocabularies. Much current research is focusing on user-independence, speech understanding (rather than simple speech recognition), sentence understanding (rather than simple word understanding), and the ability to handle vocabularies approaching those in human users (typically around 5000 words).

Other research is focusing on the machine recognition of *handwriting* (again single letters are easier to recognise than whole words or sentences). Some handwriting recognition systems do not rely on an inspection of the finished words but monitor the writing movement: it is possible, for example, to recognise signatures by charting the changes in direction and accelerations and decelerations in the speed of a person's writing.

People can also communicate by drawing diagrams, moving their hands to signal directions or to identify an object, and by various other manual techniques. Computer techniques are being developed to match these human modes. For example, a *light pen* allows a user to draw directly onto a screen, with the drawn lines or diagrams stored for future use; an electric pen can be used to draw on a specially-prepared *graphics tablet* in front of a screen to signal required colours and shapes; and a *digitising tablet* can be used to translate complex drawings into a computerised form. Some systems allow communication with a computer by the user simply touching the screen with a finger: *touch-sensitive screens* may employ an array of infra-red light beams in front of the screen, or thin wires carried behind a flexible screen sheet. *Joysticks* and *trackerballs* can be used to control a cursor which moves on the screen to indicate where the next input is to be made. A *mouse,* with wheels, moves on a flat surface to control the screen cursor;

and a *cat,* a touch sensitive pad, allows movement of the operator's fingers to control the cursor.

Pictures, whether moving or still, can be converted into a digital form and fed into the computer. In *facsimile transmission,* for example, a document is scanned, converted into a digital code, and fed along a communications link to a device which interprets the code to re-create the picture. Still or moving pictures from a camera can also be digitised and then processed: robot 'eyes' can be induced to understand scenes in this way.

A computer may output information on a display screen (a visual display unit typically uses a cathode ray tube for this purpose, though flat screens have now been developed to overcome the bulkiness of a crt), or directly to printers for the generation of hard-copy documents. Computers may also, as we have observed, talk back to a human operator by synthesising speech. Synthetic sounds and digitised voices can be used to provide voice output: voices can be generated, and music and other sound effects can be produced. The basic speech sounds *phonemes,* can be re-created using sound generators. Software is being developed to combine the phonemes into natural speech rhythms. Today it is already possible to synthesis male and female voices and to provide them with regional accents. Voice response, the output corollary to voice recognition, may be expected to become an increasingly important element in fifth-generation research.

FIFTH-GENERATION RESEARCH

A principal objective in the fifth-generation programme is to develop an intelligent man/machine interface to enhance the user-friendliness of systems. In the 1970s much research was initiated in this area, associated with such topics as artificial intelligence, computational linguistics and pattern recognition. Fifth-generation research may be expected to build on this work to develop flexible interactive facilities. The defined plan for developing an intelligent man/machine interface comprises three fundamental categories:

— natural language processing;

— speech processing;

— picture and image processing.

Hozumi Tanaka et al (1981), outlining the fifth-generation scheme use the term 'intelligent man/machine interface system' to denote a front-end processor for input/output using spoken and written natural language and pictures and images.

It is recognised that the larger the number of users becomes, the greater will be the need for a natural language processing capability (this is seen as a very difficult computational task). Table 7 shows the fifth-generation specification for a natural language processing language. A number of primitive techniques are being developed in the research on natural language processing:

— determination of a basic vocabulary in each application domain;

— creation of a text database in each application domain;

— development of a flexible parser;

— development of grammar rules;

— morpheme and syntactic analysis;

— sentence generation;

— semantic analysis;

— pragmatic analyses;

— natural language processing machine.

In the experience of Tanaka et al (1981), more than 80 per cent of all natural language texts (in Japanese) are accounted for by 2,000 most frequently occurring words. For this reason, a basic vocabulary of less than 5,000 words is deemed sufficient. In the initial research stage currently under way, the parsing techniques based on the logic programming developed at Edinburgh University are being investigated. These techniques facilitate the implementation of augmented context-free grammar rules in a natural way. One aim is to enhance PROLOG to produce an effective nucleus (or kernel) language. Such topics as sentence generation, semantic analysis and programmatic analysis will be investigated in the later stages of research. Aspects of natural language and speech processing, as envisaged for the basic application systems, are shown in Figure 5.1.

Languages	Japanese, English, . . .
Vocabulary size	Depends on application: For front-end processing of question answering system; 5,000 – 10,000 words. For text data processing; more than 50,000 words.
Number of grammar rules	Less than 2,000.
Application domains	Front-end processor of question answering system: Information retrieval, computer aided instruction, medical consultation, decision support system, . . . Text data processing: Scientific literature, technical manuals, newspapers, . . . Machine translation.
Processing speed	0.05 sec. for each sentence (of 25 words) (including both syntactic and semantic processing).
Accuracy	99% of input sentences parsed correctly in syntactic processing without human intervention (post editing, etc).

Table 7   Specification for Natural Language Processing System

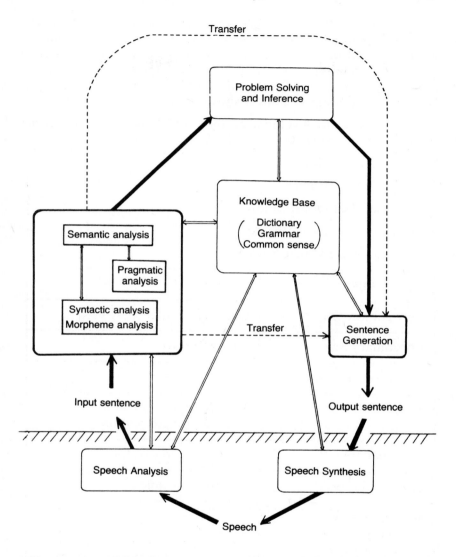

Figure 5.1 Natural Language and Speech Processing in Basic Application Systems
(Source: *Proceedings of International Conference on Fifth-Generation Computer Systems,* 19-22 October, 1981, JIPDEC)

Speech recognition systems have been in practical use for some time, though usually based on simple word recognition in a limited vocabulary. More advanced systems will be developed for fifth-generation computers. The target specification for a speech processing system, to be developed in conjunction with a natural language processing system, is shown in Table 8.

It is necessary to develop a number of techniques in connection with research into speech processing:

— speech analysis;

— feature extraction;

— phoneme classification;

— basic speech synthesis;

— database of speech wave;

Speech Input	
Recognition Object	Continuous speech
Vocabulary Size	50,000 words
Word Recognition Rate	95%
Speaker	Multiple speakers with moderate adaptation
Pronunciation	Accurate and careful
Processing Speed	3 times real time
Speech Output	
Vocabulary Size	50,000 words
Speech Synthesis	Synthesis by rule

Table 8   Specification of Speech Processing System

— adaptation of tuning methods for individual speaker differences;

— spoken sentence understanding;

— Japanese (and other natural language) speech output;

— hardware system for speech understanding;

— intelligent speech interface system.

Current research is focusing on speech analysis, feature extraction and basic speech synthesis methods. During the later research stages, attention will be directed at the adaptation or tuning methods for individual speaker differences, and at the development of the necessary hardware system. During the final stages of research, efforts will be made to develop: a spoken-sentence understanding system, a speech application system, including a voice-activated typewriter and a voice dialogue system. Research into natural language processing may be expected to contribute to the development of a prototype intelligent speech interface system.

Research into speech understanding will focus on acoustic level processing (starting with speech analysis and leading to the classification of phonemes) and on language level processing (where the results of acoustic processing allow speech to be understood). The main problem in acoustic level processing, peculiar to speech, is how to translate speech waves into phoneme sequences. At the level of language processing, a phoneme lattice is interpreted to yield an understanding of the speech. This is similar to, but more difficult than, natural language processing: the processing starts with a phoneme lattice (that carries inevitable uncertainties) rather than from a reliable character string.

The intelligent man/machine interface will also provide facilities in which a user can handle pictures and image data (image-oriented knowledge is usually composed of spatial features described in a symbolic form). Pictorial and image data will be stored, processed and retrieved as a knowledge base. One aim will be to allow image-understanding and image-oriented application studies (eg in CAD/CAM, aerial and satellite uses, chest X-ray image analysis, etc) to be performed efficiently. Here the research

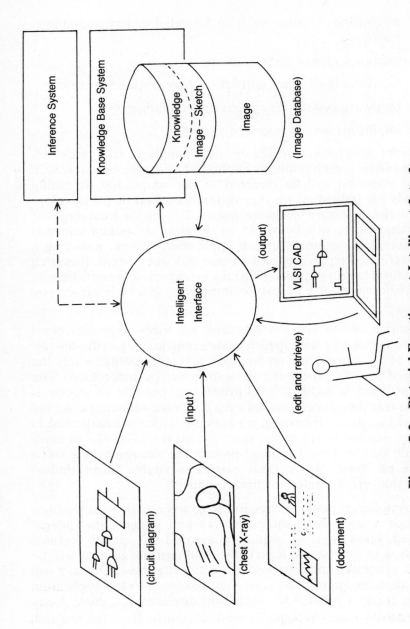

Figure 5.2　Pictorial Functions at Intelligent Interface
(Source: *Proceedings of the International Conference on Fifth-Generation Computer Systems,*
19-22 October 1981, JIPDEC)

goals are intended to relate to using two-dimensional signal data as a knowledge source, inputting pictorial and image data and outputting after processing, demonstrating practical uses (eg in VLSI CAD systems and X-ray image analysis, etc), and providing an intelligent knowledge-acquisition subsystem. Figure 5.2 shows the intelligent man/machine interface from the viewpoint of the image database system.

Various techniques will need to be developed to achieve an intelligent man/machine interface with the required functions. The following necessary techniques are regarded as stand-alone functions which will facilitate incremental system development and integration:

— *intelligent data input,* to input pictorial and image data at high-speed;

— *image-sketch-relation conversion,* to extract features (such as shape, grey level, texture, etc) and structures. The sketches are stored in a relational knowledge base;

— *efficient image storage,* to compress the original two-dimensional data to efficient codes where necessary;

— *flexible data manipulation,* to manage the databases;

— *intelligent data output,* to reconstruct images from sketches and from compressed data in the display console;

— *high-level control,* to control the various functions by means of high-level control languages.

In the experimental stage, research is being conducted into high-level languages and into the hardware of feature extractors, display generators, and the image database engine. At the pilot model implementation stage, a small-scale intelligent interface will be integrated with the associated hardware in conjunction with the inference machine and the knowledge base machine. At the prototype implementation stage, a full-scale intelligent interface will be implemented. Information will be available on practical applications (eg reorganising handwriting for VLSI CAD and facilitating X-ray analysis for medical consultation). Figure 5.3 shows the relationships and the internal operations of the three subsystems in an application system.

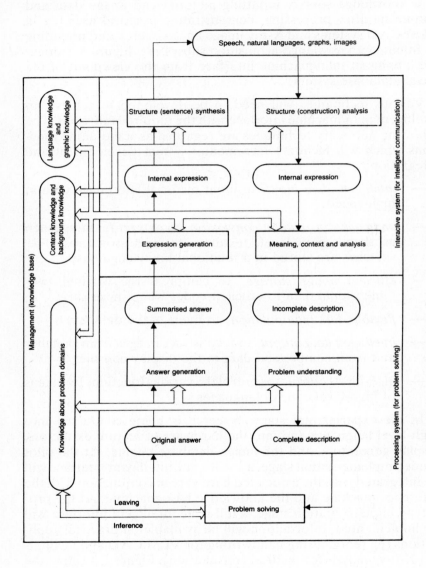

Figure 5.3 Subsystems in an Application System

This section has outlined some of the main elements in the fifth-generation research aimed at developing an intelligent man/machine interface. In the main, these have related to such topics as natural language processing, speech processing and the processing of pictorial and image data. Fifth-generation research will draw on established work in these areas. Some highlights and developments are profiled in the remainder of this chapter under three main heads: Natural Language Processing, Aural Communication (to include Voice Recognition and Speech Synthesis), and Visual Perception (to highlight, for example, the use of cameras in artificial systems for pattern recognition).

NATURAL LANGUAGE PROCESSING

A main aim of artificial intelligence is to develop systems capable of understanding natural language (see Chapter 3). The fifth-generation aim of developing systems that are highly user-friendly suggests that the current high-level computer languages are inadequate for many purposes: they have to be learned (ie they are not 'high-level' enough). A corollary to this interpretation is that natural languages (French, Japanese, English, Russian, etc) will become the ultimate programming languages, assuming that sufficiently intelligent man/machine interfaces can be designed.

Research into natural language systems can be traced to the 'mechanical translation' programs of the 1950s, with research drawing today on such topics as psychology, linguistics and the philosophy of language. Some conversational systems (see Actual Expert Systems, Chapter 4) accept queries and comments typed in English on a standard keyboard. The functioning natural language systems are still less flexible than normal English and make more demands on the user. Normal English tends to be verbose, poorly structured, logically loose, etc: a user of a natural language system is required to exert more self-discipline.

Furthermore what appears to be a tight, well-defined statement in normal English may turn out under scrutiny to be semantically ambiguous. A natural language system requires a weighty back-up of information (knowledge) to discriminate soundly between two equally tenable meanings, only one of which is intended. The necessary encoding of this specialised knowledge can limit the portability of the systems. Kaplan and Ferris (1982) have noted that the considerable expertise required to encode domain-specific knowledge 'has severely limited the distribution of natural language systems and is likely to continue to do so'. Another problem is that the database needs to be updated periodically, a circumstance that may involve the introduction of vocabulary unknown to the system.

It is also emphasised that if natural language systems are prone to error (because of the ambiguities in normal English), they can be hazardous in critical applications. A misinterpretation can obviously occur where the user's intention differs from the system's understanding of the communication. This danger may be encouraged by the similarity of English-like systems to normal English: users may be tempted to use natural expressions (which in some cases are logically vague). The best known natural language system, already mentioned is Intellect (formerly Robot) of the Artificial Intelligence Corporation, Mass, but various other natural language systems are emerging (eg Hewlett-Packard is considering one for its desk-top computers).

One purpose of fifth-generation research will be to overcome the limitations of existing natural language systems. It will also be necessary to develop facilities for voice input using natural language: the user will be able to talk to the computer (or computer-controlled system) using his or her own language, and the computer will understand and respond (possibly using speech synthesis facilities). Such facilities will depend upon research findings in various fields: for example, knowledge representation, semantic nets, etc (see Tennant, 1978). Today natural language research is moving beyond the analysis of words and other symbols to analysis of the world in which the words have meaning. For words to be fully understood – by person or machine – it is necessary to interpret the words in the context of the appropriate knowledge framework. This is partly a cognitive matter, with direct relevance to aspects of psychology and artificial intelligence.

Most natural language systems have developed to understand words fed into a computer system via a keyboard. Today much research is also being directed at developing systems that can understand spoken words and sentences, and which can then synthesise their own spoken responses. Much of this work has been conducted outside the mainstream fifth-generation computer programme but will obviously contribute to it. Effective voice-recognition and speech-synthesis systems must represent the ulti-mate goal of research into user-friendly computers.

AURAL COMMUNICATION

Voice Recognition

For several years, efforts have been made to enable computers to recognise spoken words. For example, the Voice Data Input Ter-minal from the Nippon Electricity Company was launched in 1978. This three-processor terminal was able to recognise up to 120 words, spoken without pause in groups of up to five words. Threshold Technology Inc of Delran, N J, introduced voice recog-nition units using 16-bit LSI-11 microcomputers in 1976. The Threshold model 600 was able to recognise continuous speech.

Typically the NEC terminal included a voice analyser, a refer-ence pattern memory, and three microprocessors required to per-form programming, input/output, and control functions. In this configuration the pattern-matching processor, a high-speed bipo-lar assemblage of mostly transistor-transistor-logic (TTL) devices, matches the patterns of incoming speech with those stored in the reference pattern memory. The I/O processor is the interface between the voice recognition system and remote-control units serving two operator positions. This processor also handles input from a tape reader that provides the words to be stored. Recogni-tion in this system is complete 300 milliseconds after the end of the word group, allowing an input of up to 60 words a minute. The Threshold 600 achieved recognition in a similar time with a voc-abulary of less than 100 words but required up to one second when the full 512 word vocabulary was used.

It is now acknowledged that speech recognition units 'can per-form flawlessly wherever the computer expects a specific input' (Scott, 1983). The computer is required simply to verify that a specific input has been received. Recognition still relies upon matching an unknown utterance against a number of known utter-ances, and then selecting the best match. Hence recognition units require facilities for effective acoustic analysis, data reduction techniques, and efficient pattern-matching algorithms. High-performance speech-recognition units use linear productive coding (LPC) for acoustic analyses, and dynamic programming (DP) for pattern matching. These techniques have tended to be expensive to implement but costs are falling.

An alternative to dynamic programming (nonlinear time warping) is linear time compression. For example, in the Scott Instruments VET series, an utterance of up to 1.5 seconds is divided into eight equal parts, and an interpolated point at each of the spacings is stored as part of a template. A spectral histogram is generated to compensate for durational differences of utterances. This approach can allow even small computers to perform effective recognition tasks. An Apple computer, for instance, using linear time compression as a background program to a VET system, can perform real-time recognition with fast response time – typically within 200 milliseconds of the completion of the utterance, even in circumstances where the full vocabulary is employed.

The smaller the required vocabulary, the easier it is to design a reliable and effective recognition system. If a large vocabulary is needed for a particular application the user must be prepared to spend time teaching the machine how to respond. And even then, with current technology, there are various impediments to accurate recognition. *Word verification* methods have been developed to improve the efficiency of the recognition process.

The verification approach is based on the 1-word vocabulary, ie only one word or phrase is acceptable at a time, the aim being to verify the active word, not to select the correct word from among many, as is attempted in most speech recognition systems. More processing time and more interpretive data can be focused on the single word, with limitations on the total vocabulary size determined by the amount of mass storage available. An experimental system called voice-aided wirewrapping (described by Scott, 1983) uses the word verification approach.

In the Scott Instruments VBLS system, which also uses word verification, training the system is regarded as an essential part of the user's learning process. For instance, the system can be trained in foreign languages by functioning in a conventional way in a language laboratory: when a student hears a word from a tape recorder, he repeats it and the utterance is used by the computer as a training template. This type of application is one of many that will influence fifth-generation research into the development of intelligent interfaces.

By the late-1970s it was obvious that speech recognition systems were a practical possibility for various applications. Voice control in the industrial environment was seen as particularly useful where (Welch, 1980):

— the worker's hands are busy;

— mobility is required during the data entry process;

— the worker's eyes must remain fixed upon a display, an optical instrument, or some object to be tracked;

— the environment is too harsh to allow use of a keyboard.

Specific industrial applications for voice-recognition systems were identified for such areas as quality control, incoming inspection, receiving accountability, part and serial number verification, warehousing and sorting. In the early 1980s, voice data entry was being used in such CAD/CAM applications as text annotation in printed circuit board component layout, preparation of program tapes for NC machine tools, and generation of wire lists, civil engineering drawings, structural drawings, and bills of material. Voice input was also being used in the office environment.

In general the performance of word-recognition systems has been measured by three parameters:

— *accuracy*. It has been found that poor accuracy quickly discourages user involvement, without which it is difficult to improve operating systems. Word-recognition accuracies below 95 per cent cause frustration and, in practical terms, the data flow may be seriously impaired. Various working systems in the early-1980s boasted accuracies greater than 98 per cent;

— *vocabulary size*. With an increase in vocabulary size it is often difficult to maintain accuracy. In fact, accuracy is at its best in speaker-dependent, isolated-word systems operating with small vocabularies carrying few similar-sounding word pairs ('confusion pairs'). It is easier to extend the vocabulary if most of the words are polysyllabic, making it easier to avoid confusion;

— *data entry speed*. Many applications, in industry and elsewhere, require vocabularies of 50 words or less, but available systems may offer data entry speeds that are marginal or even inadequate. In general, continuous-speech recognition systems provide faster throughput than isolated-word systems, but often at the expense of accuracy. In fast continuous speech, adjacent words modify each other, an effect termed 'coarticulation', so that individual words may no longer match the reference templates.

In 1980, IBM researchers at Yorktown Heights, NY, used a computer to transcribe spoken sentences from a 1000-word vocabulary read at a normal speaking pace. The sentences were transformed into hard copy with 91 per cent accuracy, believed at that time to be the best obtained under complex experimental conditions. Use was made of an IBM System/370 Model 168 computer with high fidelity equipment. The user talked into a microphone, and the words recognised by the computer appeared on a screen.

This work, reported by Dr Frederick Jelinek at the 1980 SAE Congress in Detroit, was based on a 1000-word natural vocabulary drawn from sentences used by lawyers in submitting US patent applications in the laser field. The entire laser patent text embraced a vocabulary of 12,000 words, reduced by computer search to the most frequently used 1000 to enable the recognition experimentation to be carried out.

Progress towards cost-effective voice-recognition systems has been influenced by the development of high levels of computer power at reducing costs. In common with other electronic systems, recognition units are beginning to exploit VLSI technology to achieve high-performance, relatively low-cost results. By the late-1970s a voice preprocessor used to convert an analogue signal from the microphone into a digital signal for processing might have occupied a 15-inch square board, whereas today (1983) such a preprocessor can be incorporated on a couple of VLSI chips.

The emergence of 32-bit and 64-bit microprocessors will also influence the development of speech-recognition systems. The increased computer power will be linked to enhanced algorithms to achieve higher levels of performance and reliability. There will be growing pressure for the development of an accurate continuous-speech algorithm, which in turn will require increased computer power. In currently available systems, trade-offs are inevitable between performance (eg vocabulary size) and cost (eg the amount of storage available), with the result that systems range from small-vocabulary, speaker-dependent units to large-vocabulary multi-user facilities. And speech output units (see Speech Synthesis, below) generate sounds ranging from robot-voice stereotypes to the most persuasive male and female voices. In 1982 it was reckoned that several thousand computer installations were using voice data input. One prediction is that by the late-1980s the market for speech recognition units will reach $100 million worldwide.

Three major areas are seen (by Lineback, 1983) as likely to boost the voice-recognition industry:

— the introduction by Intel and by Texas Instruments of various speech-transaction products;

— Votan Inc's introduction of a single-board speaker-independent speech recognition unit;

— the emergence of new development systems allowing engineers to spend less time integrating speech-recognition units with other systems.

In 1983, Intel developed its entry into voice-recognition markets with three levels of products: a development system, a speech transaction board, and a chip set. The Intel board allows up to 200 discrete utterances to be enrolled, each lasting up to 2.2 seconds, and recognises discrete utterances only, with 80 to 240 milliseconds' pause between commands. The Votan 6000 recognition unit will initially be marketed for a language profile that Stu Farnham, director of international marketing, calls the American dialect.

At the (December 1982) Midcon show in Dallas, Texas Instruments described work on a single-board, speaker-dependent word recogniser, a prototype indicating (for example) the algorithms that TI deems to be important. The prototype can recognise about 50 words, the average item lasting 0.6 second. It is possible to string words together to form phrases: a single utterance may contain a string of up to 21 connected vocabulary items.

The TI approach uses the digital extraction of linear-predictive-coding parameters, based on a model of human speech. The parameters are used to characterise words and data is passed into the memory for future reference. The system extracts the parameters from heard speech and performs computations to determine similarities between the spoken words and the stored templates. The algorithm, in common with algorithms in other systems, also carries out nonlinear time-warping to compensate for speed variations in human speech. As with other systems, software is a key consideration (see, for example, Iverson et al, 1982; Chan and Lee, 1982).

One of the most successful voice-recognition systems is the Logos system, developed by Logica using techniques designed by the Government's Joint Speech Research Unit (JSRU). Logos, designed for continuous speech, allows extensive real-time processing to take place according to word sequencing rules adapted to particular applications. A Logica brochure highlights various Logos features:

— continuous recognition of natural speech in real time for vocabularies of up to several hundred words:

— fully user-programmable word sequence rules (syntax) also allowing the incorporation of error correction strategies;

— special 'wildcard' templates to permit keyword spotting, and to eliminate spurious input (such as coughs);

— sophisticated acoustic analysis which reduces sensitivity to variations in microphone position and background noise;

— a powerful microcomputer to run applications-specific programs in high- or low-level language and to handle interfacing to the user and host machines;

— highly modular design allowing flexibility in configuration for small or large vocabularies and simple or complex applications.

Logos represents a significant advance over most other word recognition systems, allowing continuous recognition of spoken phrases of any length from a predefined vocabulary. This requirement demands extensive resort to parallel computing; otherwise, the recognition process, unable to keep pace with the speech rate, would not be able to operate in real time. To handle large vocabularies, a split is made so that central sets of computing for sections of the vocabulary are individually handled by a separate dynamic programming processor, each being based on a standard Intel 8086 microprocessor working on a 16-bit basis. Similar micros are used for the control processor, designed to handle interactions between templates and to supervise first-stage signal capture and analysis.

The word-sequencing rules (syntax) can be used to reduce the number of word choices at any point in a phrase, so reducing the amount of computation needed and in some cases improving the recognition accuracy. The syntax also includes error-correction strategies. Rule 'nodes' are each connected to a word or groups of alternative words allowed at that point.

Nodes can be looped together to allow the words between them to be recognised any number of times: in a simple case all the digits may be allowed between two looped nodes, thus allowing the operator to speak a digit sequence of any length. Recognition results are fed out either at the end of a phrase or on a continuous basis a word or so behind the current utterance.

Logos can be controlled by a VDU or host computer. Users are individually required to train the machine by speaking one example of each word in the defined vocabulary; where a VDU is used, the operator is prompted with each word when the training mode is selected. The reference patterns obtained during training can be stored. The functional operation of Logos is shown in Figure 5.4 (spectrum analysis being initially performed on microphone input).

Logos uses algorithms developed at JSRU and includes a facility for programming syntax in the form of a finite state grammar with

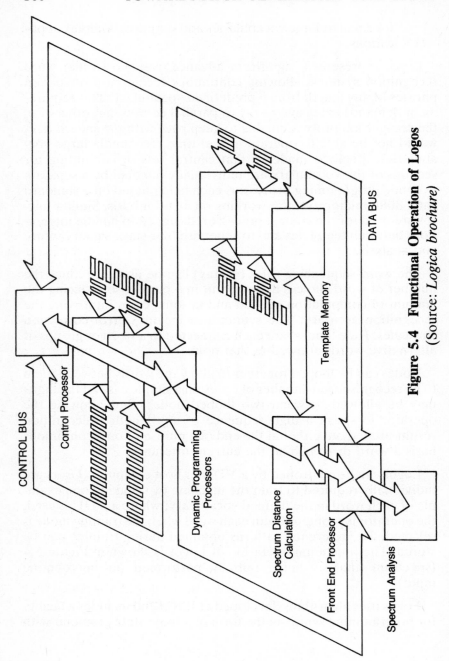

Figure 5.4 Functional Operation of Logos
(Source: *Logica brochure*)

loops. The method of acoustic analysis incorporates such features as noise compensation, spectrum shape normalisation and variable frame rate analysis designed to improve the recognition performance. The high degree of flexibility and programmability make Logos a powerful tool for applications requiring connected or continuous speech input. There is scope for extending Logos for multi-speaker use. It is expected that the system will be increasingly relevant to applications in such areas as information retrieval from computer databases, data entry to computers, programming of NC machine tools, CAD, office automation, and the direct control of training simulators.

The Logos system represents one impressive member of the growing family of voice recognition units. In themselves, such systems are not part of the fifth-generation research programme. However, they will manifestly contribute to the central fifth-generation objective of developing user-friendly systems.

Speech Synthesis

Speech synthesis is the other side of the aural communication coin. What we find is that many companies specialising in voice recognition systems are also interested in speech synthesis. This seems reasonable enough: a friendly computer may be able to hear us and print out a reply, but the system may seem even friendlier if it can answer with spoken words. And we should not be surprised to learn that there are common techniques in voice recognition and speech synthesis: linear-predictive-coding* for example, has relevance to both.

In 1978 a speech synthesiser chip, the TMC 0280, appeared with the TMC 0350 read-only memory and the TMC 0270 controller in the Speak & Spell learning aid from Texas. This was one of the first speech synthesis chips based on the (then) recently discovered voice-compression technique of linear-predictive-coding. When the system produces speech, the controller specifies to the synthesiser the starting point of a string of data stored in the memory. The 131,072-bit ROM can accommodate 165 words, it ouput providing the pitch, amplitude and filter parameters from which the synthesiser chip constructs the speech waveform.

---

* For a description of LPC, see Brightman and Crook, 1982.

The TMC 0280 system (described by Wiggins and Brantingham, 1978) was one of a number heralding 'yet another phase of electronic wizardry'. In 1978 it was easy to see the practical possibilities of speaking clocks, machines that could explain their operations in spoken words, and computers with which conversation would be feasible using natural language. And at that time it was discerned that voice recognition (see above) would prove a weightier problem than speech synthesis.

The late-1970s saw a range of products that could synthesise their own speech in response to queries or other inputs. Votrax of Michigan, a division of Federal Screw Works, developed portable speech synthesisers for the vocally impaired, and began manufacturing a Business Communicator which was able to translate up to 64 telephone Touch-Tone inputs into an audio response. A multilingual voice system, at first synthesising English and German, was also developed. Master Specialities Company, California, manufactured a talking calculator and a variety of word-oriented announcement products. Similarly, Telesensory Systems Inc, again in California, launched a talking calculator for the blind.

It was also suggested (eg by Miller, 1979) that speech recognition would replace Touch-Tone telephone input, by (perhaps) the mid-1980s, as the preferred input capability to computer systems, and that a wide range of systems would be able to talk back to the human user. For example, a voice recognition/voice response system was launched by Dialog Systems Inc as a general purpose facility with wide application in food, pharmacy, credit verification, telephone paging, etc. With such a system, the computer can detect an input error and ask the caller to repeat, for example, a credit card number for verification. In some circumstances the computer can read a number back to a caller to ask if it is correct: if the caller confirms, the computer then checks its files. The Dialog system responds to a caller in a male voice recorded on an optical soundtrack revolving on a drum, and can understand male and female voices. A 1978 report from the New York Quantum Science Corporation observed: 'The long-term trend will be to accommodate human rather than machine characteristics, resulting in the ever increasing use of speech as a machine input/output medium in industry, office and home applications'.

By 1980, IBM had launched an Audio Typing Unit, using voice synthesis techniques to provide a variety of functions for blind typists. The speech was created when basic speech sounds (phonemes) were combined according to an extensive set of pronunciation rules stored in the units memory. In theory this allowed for an unlimited vocabulary: sounds could be synthesised in any combination. Furthermore, the unit blended and modified the phoneme commands for transitions, pauses and rhythm (see *Software Digest,* 8/11/79).

The necessary complexity of speech synthesis has often been highlighted by consideration of the human vocal tract (with reference to lungs, trachea, vocal cords, epiglottis, velum, tongue, nasal pharynx, etc). This serves to illustrate the many phonetic elements present in ordinary spoken words. Machines that talk are necessarily required to exhibit a comparable vocal flexibility.

For example, speech may simply be recorded digitally and called up when required. Orr (1979) highlighted an early stock ordering/availability system for garages that operated on this principle. This approach can produce high-quality speech but is very heavy on memory. Other techniques are more economic on memory but require more sophisticated software. For example, the ANGLOPHONE software sold by Upper Case was used by the early Votrax and Computalker speech synthesisers to convert normal spelling into phonetic code.

Some early speech synthesisers were intended as commercial products for education or domestic use. We have mentioned Speak & Spell as a learning (and teaching) aid, and talking calculators have been available for several years. Linggard and Marlow (1979) describe a low-cost, programmable digital speech synthesiser used for research purposes: this device has a general-purpose architecture which enables it to simulate formant-type synthesisers as well as vocal-track models, and all in real time. Two hundred integrated circuits were used at a cost (in 1979) of £350. A principal use of the machine was to compare different synthesiser types.

In 1980 Votrax announced a single-chip speech synthesiser, the SC-01, having as major features unlimited vocabulary and minimal memory requirements. With this product, neither the chip supplier nor a human speaker is required to assist in generating a vocabulary. Phonemes are stored as 6-bit words in a separate memory chip, with the speech integrated circuit containing the circuits for selecting the phonemes and connecting them to generate the necessary words (and other sounds).

In some applications, the synthesiser chip independently accesses the stored phonemes. When the reproduced phrases reach a certain complexity (eg if words to be spoken go beyond a simple phrase), a microprocessor is used to control the synthesis task. The LSI chip was designed for Votrax by Silicon Systems Inc (Bassak, 1980), and Intelligent Systems Corp, maker of small business systems, developed a voice-synthesis peripheral based on the SC-01 circuit. 1980 also saw the launch by National Semiconductor Corp of its first speech-synthesis chips (LeBoss, 1980).

By the early-1980s, speech synthesis applications were evident in a wide range of industrial, commercial and educational sectors. Samuel (1981) describes the use of a microprocessor and a speech synthesiser which together can detect system faults and then make a telephone call to summon assistance. Research has suggested that voice response is more effective than flashing lights or video displays. In this system the vocabulary is limited to about 1000 words (larger vocabularies are possible but involve some loss of speech clarity). Speech synthesis of this sort allows effective contact to be maintained at all times with a remote operator. This is of particular value where system monitoring is required in hostile environments and in other circumstances where it is not convenient for an operator to be present. And, inevitably, the military has had an eye on what can be done with voice-recognition and speech-synthesis techniques (Iversen, 1980).

Today, partly under the stimulus of the fifth-generation programme, a number of approaches to speech synthesis are being researched. In summary, it is now possible to produce practical speech output by means of waveform synthesis, constructive synthesis or analysis synthesis. (The various approaches are described and compared in Brightman and Crook, 1982.)

With *waveform synthesis,* the original speech waveform is recreated by sampling the input at suitable intervals (eg at a sampling rate of 8 KHz, yielding data rates ranging from 64K to 96K per second). The typical rates tend to make unaided waveform synthesis impractical because too much data needs to be stored. Storage requirements can be significantly reduced by developing an electronic model of the vocal tract controlled by parameters derived from raw input data. The Texas Instruments LPC technique, for example, models the vocal tract by means of a 10-pole, time-varying, digital lattice filter. Here the bit rate of the coded data for pitch, energy level and the filter parameters is up to 100 times lower than that required for waveform synthesis. (The LPC approach is highly suited to representing the human vocal equipment.)

In *constructive synthesis,* speech output is generated from a library of token sounds under the control of a set of stored rules. For example, American English can be broken up into 42 'building-block' sounds *(phonemes),* though it can be difficult to assemble such elements into natural-sounding speech. A TI approach, using the constructive synthesis method, expands the 42-phoneme family to 128 allophones, fine variations of the basic sounds. Allophonic speech is a better approximation to human speech, and there is scope for further refining the allophonic rules to achieve higher levels of naturalness.

Analysis synthesis relies on generating speech from human input. An initial step in this method may be to write the complete vocabulary for a product into a script: all the words, including their repetitions in various contexts, are used. Then, during a recording session, data is extracted from a speaker's reading of the script. During LPC analysis, data is transformed from direct analogues of speech waveforms to LPC-10 parameters which are then fed into a synthesiser chip. The data can be edited to improve the final sound quality. In this way, the analysis-synthesis approach accurately preserves the character of human speech.

The various methods of computer-generated speech are variants of two broad approaches – playback and synthesis (Foss, 1982). These are reflected in the growing range of computer-based products with speech capability. Wickersham et al (1982) emphasise how digital speech-compression-and-synthesis technology has aided the development of products that can talk to their human users (reference is made to the Digitalker preprogrammed speech-synthesis system and to the use of speech editors enabling low-volume users to create their own vocabularies). A recent product from National Semiconductor, the BLC-8281 add-in speech-processor board, allows OEMs to convert their microcomputer development stations into speech editors.

Synthesised speech will offer increasing opportunities to enhance the intelligence of the interfaces between machines and human users. In the industrial environment, machine-spoken words may be more effective than flashing lights and alarm bells: a greater quantity of information can be conveyed in a more acceptable manner. Talking meters, for example, can be useful in badly lit locations. And speech synthesis facilities can be useful in offices, public address systems, aircraft, etc. Some of the areas in which voice systems can be employed are listed in Table 9.

Industry:	machine control, alarms, advisory systems, process control, instrumentation, dark-room aids, etc.
Offices:	typewriter and word processor control, operation of information systems, multi-purpose workstations, copiers etc
Transport:	dashboard meters, aircraft control, warning systems, information systems, etc
Telecomms:	answering machines, private exchanges, security alarms, information systems, etc
Consumer:	kitchen appliances, toys, door 'bells', aids for the handicapped, calculators, banking terminals, retailing facilities, etc
Computer:	personal systems, expert (consultation) systems in medicine or science, commercial management aids, etc

Table 9   Some Application Areas for Voice Systems

Technological developments will allow for an increased range of speech-synthesis uses. Fred Wickersham, marketing manager for National Semiconductor, has observed that anyone with a system that runs CP/M (the most popular operating system for 8-bit microprocessors) will soon be able to build a vocabulary for a speech synthesiser using a standard set of words: 'We will be providing a vocabulary of about 1000 words and the software to transfer the words into [the CP/M-based computer's] random-access memory from a set of CP/M-compatible diskettes. The customer can then pick words and arrange them into the phrases he needs' (quoted in *Electronics,* 8/9/82). And the emerging facilities will not be limited to a single natural language. XCOM, a small French firm, has developed a speech synthesis system, based on the CP-S100 card, which can convert text input into natural-sounding French speech output.

Growing attention is being given to both voice-recognition and speech-synthesis facilities. Phil Manchester (1982) recently surveyed the product innovations at Compec (pointing out, incidentally, the relevance of expert-systems research to effective voice understanding facilities). Again we may emphasise the importance of aural communication systems in rendering computers more user-friendly, a central fifth-generation goal.

VISUAL PERCEPTION

The development of visual capacities may be represented as a means of enhancing the computer ability to recognise patterns in the environment. We have already seen (Chapter 3) that pattern recognition is a key element in artificial intelligence and, as such, likely to influence the evolution of fifth-generation computers. Artificial vision will feature in a growing number of technological innovations: for example, robots are developing 'eyes' (along with other senses) which, when linked to the sort of computer capabilities being developed for expert systems, will assist machines in their efforts to behave intelligently in a changing environment.

As with modes of aural communication, artificial vision has existed as an element in practical technology for several years. For example, in 1976 the American Auto-Place company introduced the Opto-sense vision facility in standard robots; a 1977 application used a robot for the visual inspection of transmission separator plates; and in 1978 the SIGHT-1 system was introduced at the General Motors Delco Electronics Division to check the position of transistor chips being assembled in high-energy ignition systems.

As early as 1974, patents were being issued in Japan for tactile, internal measurement and visual sensors, with a clear trend towards visual sensor research in subsequent years. Hitachi has introduced vidicon cameras for shape recognition and positioning of transistors in die bonding, and for remote inspection of nuclear plants. Such cameras are also built into robots by Mitsubishi for shape recognition and positioning with assembly tasks and transistor die bonding; by Yasukawa for arc welding applications; and by Kawasaki Heavy Industries for assembly operations. Onda and Ohashi (1979), Agin (1980) and Jarvis (1980) describe the use of artificial vision inspection techniques in various industrial contexts.

The recognition of simple patterns and positions in assembly and other industrial tasks represents one of the first stages is equipping computers with vision. A camera collects the necessary data and a computer is used to interpret it. This can be an immensely difficult task where complex modes of pattern recognition are required. One system, the UK-developed Wisand, can recognise human faces within three seconds (reported in *Computer Weekly,* 17-24/12/81), and can be used for robot vision systems, to provide handprint input to computers, and for security applications. To date, pattern recognition by computer has been used in various fields: we have mentioned robotics and industrial inspection, and uses have also been found in the processing of satellite and space images and in medicine (Myers, 1980, describes uses in connection with industry, medicine and space).

One problem in computer viscon, as with other types of artificial perception, is that the data is often incomplete. Where this happens with human visual perception, we 'fill in' the gaps, drawing on our knowledge base to generate expectations and estimate probabilities (this again emphasises the relevance of knowledge engineering and knowledge representation in the development of artificial perception). Dixon (1979) highlights the desirability, for some applications, of producing programs that can accept imperfect data. One conclusion is that a pattern recognition system, appropriately configured, can perform well even when significant amounts of data are missing ('With 30 per cent blanks inserted into the data, recognition scores will typically drop by five to 15 per cent'). This type of work, particularly when allied to developments in fuzzy and kindred logics, may be seen as a further attempt to make computers more humanlike in their capabilities and performance. Jain and Haynes (1982) discuss the development of computer vision systems in connection with fuzzy set theory, and they quote Zadeh:

> 'In general, complexity and precision bear an inverse relation to one another in the sense that, as the complexity of a problem increases, the possibility of analyzing it in precise terms diminishes. Thus 'fuzzy' thinking may not be deplorable, after all, if it makes possible the solution of problems which are much too complex for precise analysis.'

This observation has a general relevance, but Jain and Haynes present a dynamic scene system, a visual facility, to illustrate the concept. They conclude that computer vision systems 'should exploit approximate reasoning, opportunistic procrastination, and knowledge (both domain-dependent and domain-independent)'. Such an approach may be expected to influence the development of vision systems for a wide range of applications.

Robotics applications will continue to proliferate as vision systems become more competent. For example, many robot vision developments were described at the Second International Conference on Robot Vision and Sensory Controls (held in Stuttgart, 2-4/11/82). These included:

— robot with camera to detect material defects;

— vision used in embroidered motif orientation in textiles;

— vision used to aid automatic insertion in printed circuit board;

— optical systems for location of objectives;

— visual feedback for robot arc welding;

— advances in automated visual inspection;

— visual system to aid the avoidance of collision in a robot environment.

Jarvis (1982) describes a robotics laboratory for the development of robot vision and other facilities ('computer vision appears to offer the richest source of sensory information for intelligent robotic manipulation in the widest range of environments'). And the December 1982 issue of *Computer,* devoted wholly to 'Robotics and Automation', carries four articles (out of a total of six) on vision systems.

McCormick et al, contributing to the 1981 Conference on Fifth-Generation Computer Systems, explore the requirements for a cognitive architecture devoted to computer vision. (It is suggested that the principles of cognitive computation described can be generalised to other types of sensory and information-processing tasks.)

An important element in the cognitive approach to artificial vision is the extent to which it draws on knowledge of human visual processing. There is frequent reference, for example, to the columnar structure of the neocortex: about a million hypercolumns, each a 'biological microprocessor', work in parallel to process visual, auditory and other data. This type of consideration is reflected in some of the features in the proposed visual analyser (McCormick et al, 1981):

— events in time are the units of analysis, rather than a hypothetical frozen instant of a visual field;

— there must be the ability to process dynamic imagery in real time;

— a biologically-based design is compatible with advances in VLSI electronics and neuroscience;

— the biological model can be extended from perceptual to cognitive machines;

— the biological model can be realised in VLSI hardware. A three-dimensional array of functional units offers adequate computational power for real-time analysis of events.

Emphasis is given to the parallel nature of information processing in biological visual systems, and how this approach can be adopted for computer vision. A layered series of array elements, composed of vertically and laterally interacting processing elements, is seen as the best model for simulating physiological vision mechanisms. In summary, the proposed visual analyser is characterised by parallel computation, image-flow processing, three-dimensional architecture, relational database, and attention-directed processing. Practical applications are envisaged for various situations requiring the real-time analysis of complex time-varying scenes. These include robotics applications in the home, industry and resources exploration, and the management of tasks in inhospitable environments.

Developments in vision systems* will continue to focus on industrial applications, in such areas as robotics and flexible manufacturing systems (for example, the January 1983 issue of *Sensor Review* carries main articles on visual inspection and vision-aided assembly). At the same time, the development of vision capability will also continue to be relevant to the evolution of non-robotic computer systems intended to operate in a user-friendly environment.

SUMMARY

This chapter has profiled some of the computer input/output considerations relevant to the development of fifth-generation systems. It may be expected that new-generation computers will continue to use most of the traditional I/O methods, albeit in an enhanced form. They will also need the new techniques that characterise interactive working between people and machines in a highly user-friendly environment. We have seen that these focus on such techniques as natural-language understanding, voice recognition, speech synthesis and visual perception.

Most of the I/O techniques that allow systems to evolve intelligence interfaces rely on aspects of pattern recognition. The signifi-

---

* Readers requiring a detailed treatment of the AI approach to computer vision are referred to M Boden, *Artificial Intelligence and Natural Man,* Harvester, 1977, Chapters 8 and 9; and to P R Cohen and E A Feigenbaum, *The Handbook of Artificial Intelligence,* Vol. 3, Pitman, 1982, Chapter 13.

cance of this topic in traditional AI studies highlights again the contribution that artificial-intelligence research will make to the development of fifth-generation systems designed for ease-of-use by human beings. Human beings interact usefully because they individually bring their intelligence to the task. When computers are more intelligent, more humanlike, communication between people and machines will become similarly natural, straightforward and effective.

Many of the I/O techniques being developed relate directly to sensory capabilities, eg computers will hear and see (and respond by talking). Some sensory capabilities (eg touch or tactile) relate almost exclusively to robot and industrial applications – there is a growing literature on, say, 'artificial-skin' sensors, tactile probes, etc – and such sensory developments have not been surveyed here. We can however imagine ways in which other sensory modes could be relevant to computer behaviour in various circumstances. Again we can only stress a central feature of modern technology: how many seemingly disparate trends are converging to yield intelligent artificial systems.

6 The Response to Fifth Generation

INTRODUCTION

The Japanese launch of the fifth-generation research and development programme was a dramatic event for the computer industry. Computer companies throughout the world were encouraged to review their long-term marketing and research strategies, and governments were forced to consider their investment plans. The high-profile announcement of the fifth-generation scheme stimulated media comment (in, for instance, both the general and technical press), the holding of conferences, and the creation of government-backed committees.

One aspect of the Japanese approach is, seemingly, to encourage international cooperation, though it is not clear how this would work. Japan hopes to benefit from Western research but Dr Moto-oka, head of the Japanese Fifth-Generation Computer Project (and the National Project of Scientific Supercomputers) has expressed doubts about collaboration on development and manufacturing. At the 1982 Pergamon Infotech fifth-generation conference he told the journal *Computing:* 'Japan is very interested in collaborating with the UK and we believe that your country can contribute in the theoretical field, particularly in logic programming and artificial intelligence. Many UK researchers and scholars could contribute to Japan on an individual basis.' At the same time he acknowledged that it was difficult to see how UK industry could benefit from collaboration.

The principal Western response to the Japanese plans has been to see fifth-generation development as likely to intensify international commercial competition. Unless national governments invest to meet the Japanese challenge – so one argument runs – Japan will come to dominate the computer industry in one sector after another. And observers urging, for example, increased UK government support for new technology are quick to point to the scale of Japanese government involvement in its own economy. Japanese efforts are concentrating minds in governments, companies and research establishments throughout the developed world.

At the same time, it is important to keep the Japanese schemes in proportion. Shunichi Uchida, director of the fifth-generation computer project, has suggested that the scale of the programme is not as grand as some observers have supposed. For instance, the Japanese government will invest about $500 million in the project over the decade, compared with IBM's 1981 R & D expenditure of around $1,612 million. By mid-1982 the research team for the project comprised a mere 40 people, and decisions had not been taken on the hardware to be used for the basic research. And there is debate in Japan about how much money should be spent on the project (Uchida: 'We have many critics in Japan. Many manufacturers suggest we have more urgent research items'). Some critics think that there should be more government investment in networks like Decnet, where Japan is weak; other critics have other ideas for investment.

It is clear that the response to the Japanese fifth-generation programme should be influenced not only by the idealistic projections of pundits but by a national estimate of the difficulties that the programme will face over the next decade. The intended fifth-generation prototype may not emerge in the target year of 1991, but there will obviously be significant research results en route. These may or may not yield the powerful and intelligent supercomputers predicted by the enthusiasts, but they are likely to influence the shape of computers in the 1990s and beyond.

REACTION TO FIFTH GENERATION

UK Reaction

The general UK reaction to fifth generation is that this is a highly significant programme deserving a proper response. This anodyne observation develops more thrust in specific comments and observations. For example, Charles Read, director of the Inter-Bank Research Organisation and a member of the Alvey Committee (see below), has focused on the social impact of new-generation systems ('Now we are beginning to apply technology to the service industries and if labour is taken out from there, there is nowhere for it to go'). For fifth-generation computers to be socially beneficial, social objectives have to be set now, "in clear, specific and well-defined areas, not in general 'motherhood' statements that no-one can disagree with". Mr Read's speech, at the 1981 Tokyo conference, brought a guarded response from the Japanese.

At the Pergamon Infotech fifth-generation conference (December 1982), Mr Read suggested, in the same spirit, that the first products to come out of UK research into fifth-generation should have clear social objectives, such as helping people with their tax and social security problems and providing assistance in developing countries ('Simple medical expertise could be vital to district nurses in rural India as could information on how to make a tractor work in a sea of Pakistani mud'). This social emphasis accords with some of the Japanese declarations about the purposes behind fifth-generation computers (see Chapter 2).

Any realisation of fifth-generation potential presupposes that the necessary technological development will be achieved and that this will be translated into economic benefit. Read has pointed out that there may be only about 200 people in the UK equipped for the advanced work on fifth-generation systems; and Robb Wilmot, managing director of ICL, has suggested that UK responses to fifth generation may concentrate too much on the technology with insufficient attention devoted to converting the technological initiative into economic advantage. Wilmot sees the Japanese project as 'a highly innovative attempt to increase and enhance the value added component of the Japanese economy' (quoted in *Computer Weekly,* 9/12/82), emphasising that the project should not be mistaken for a purely technological initiative. A main objective for Japan is to maintain its level of economic growth.

A growing focus on new (eg data flow) architectures and logic programming facilities is part of the UK response to fifth-generation. VME (Virtual Machine Environment) has been represented as ICL's operating for fifth-generation. Wilmot has declared that the designs proposed for the fifth-generation would be 'enveloped' in VME. And British expertise in languages such as PROLOG will be useful in fifth-generation development.

Part of the UK response to fifth generation is to continue research into relevant computer configurations. For example, a *reduction* machine is being developed at Imperial College, London, and a *data flow* machine at Manchester University. John Gurd, in the Machine Dataflow Project at Manchester, believes that the data flow machine is the closest thing we in the UK have to a fifth-generation system ('It is the nearest thing that is identifiably radical and it has features that will fit into a fifth-generation machine').

The concepts relating to both reduction machines (the result of a language-driven need) and data flow machines pre-date the Japanese plans: for example, the theory on the data-flow project, expected to be complete by 1985, is funded (to the tune of around £500,000) by the Science and Engineering Research Council.

SPL Conference

One of the first Western conferences* to consider the Japanese fifth-generation was presented by SPL International in London on 8th and 9th July, 1982. Here the conference chairman Alex d'Agapeyeff described the Japanese project as a threat and the report on it as a 'technological Mein Kampf'. Further, the Japanese scheme was dubbed a 'computing Apocalypse'.

Professor Ed Feigenbaum of Stanford University saw the project as a brilliant marketing strategy, with the Japanese picking an economic point beyond the view of IBM and other US companies. But there were risks. Feigenbaum noted that: 'Despite the level of engineering technology involved, the project is based on software, and Japanese managers are not confortable with software; the project is very ambitious in terms of the state of current knowledge and carries great risk, a position which Japanese managers are normally averse to; nor is there a lot of in-depth knowledge

---

* Profiled by Mark Van Harmeleen, *Data Processing*, September 1982, p32.

engineering experience in Japan . . .' (quoted in *Computer Weekly,* 15/7/82). But if the Japanese only achieve 20 per cent of their goals, Feigenbaum observed, they could still finish up ahead of the game. He suggested that the $430 million (or thereabouts) ear-marked for fifth-generation research by the Japanese government would be more than matched by investments from Japanese indus-try. The total investment is more likely to be $1.5 billion spread over 10 years ('With the total combined spending on fifth genera-tion at $50 million a year in the US we won't be spending enough even if we double'). Herb Grosch, however, was more optimistic about Western chances, and pointed to the role of IBM.

The conference ended with a discussion of strategies to achieve the objective of fifth-generation computer systems. One observer, Colin Cook of Zynar, pointed out that little was known about IBM's plans and that fifth-generation computer systems would be the biggest computing growth area for the next twenty years. There was general recognition that the Japanese programme, for good or ill, was a highly dramatic development.

Atkinson Mission, Alvey Committee

In February 1982, Mr Kenneth Baker, Minister for Information Technology announced that the Department of Industry planned to set up a Group to study a possible collaborative research pro-gramme, involving the UK government, industry and universities, to develop information-technology products. This announcement followed a two-day conference at which a UK mission to Japan to investigate fifth-generation computers reported its conclusion to more than seventy representatives of the UK computing and elec-tronics industries. The Group came to be headed by Mr John Alvey, senior director of technology at British Telecom.

The purpose of the 1981 mission was to identify the Japanese aims and how they were to be achieved, and to investigate possible areas of effective collaboration in ways that would benefit the UK. Two main conclusions of the mission, led by Mr Reay Atkinson of the Department of Industry, were that if Britain were to maintain a presence in information technology, it is 'imperative that:

a) generally, the UK national effort is more effectively organ-ised than at present;

b)   there is a rapid concentration of those financial and other resources which are essential if the UK is going even to catch up with the Japanese in key areas such as advanced VLSI design capability.'

The Atkinson mission (and the resulting report) and the creation of the Alvey Group (or Committee) represented the first serious UK government responses to the Japanese announcements on fifth-generation. The Alvey Report (see below), published in September/October 1982, is a crucial document in this area.

US Reaction

In the view of at least one American, fifth-generation computers will not come from Japan. At the Pergamon Infotech conference, US consultant Phil Dorn claimed that the Japanese only do well in comparatively low-technology industries and lack the necessary innovative skills to lead the world in computing: 'The Japanese will not dominate the next generation even with help from intellectual dilettantes who hate IBM blindly. They have an outstanding ability for low-cost, high-volume production, but do not appear to have a great receptivity to new ideas or aptitude for high technology. It is extremely difficult to name a single major idea in computing, hardware or applications that came from a Japanese source. The only real exception is Pac-Man.' And Dorn points out that most companies are more concerned with running the business than rushing to install new technology ('Why bother with a fifth generation when we haven't been able to handle the last four?').

Saul Dinman, editor in chief of *Computer Design,* observed (in October 1982 issue) that the Japanese quest for a fifth-generation computer system could be 'the all-time sleeper for the US computer industry'. He suggests that the Japanese understand what is needed while, by contrast, in the US 'we stumble along blindly cranking out more and more hardware with little or no software support, speak blithely of the thousand or so application packages available for CP/M, and continue to toy with cute graphic gimmicks and pages of menus . . .'.

The Japanese see the fifth generation as a system that will be usable by noncomputer people, programmable by the user, and able to converse with the user while working out a solution to his or her problem ('The Japanese, cautious about where they put large amounts of government funds, have not chosen this definition of the fifth generation without believing that the end result is realisable'). In this view the US computer industry, in its response to fifth generation, is complacent and unrealistic.

The IBM response is to aim to continue its dominance 'through incremental improvements to today's computers' *(New Scientist,* 29/7/82). For example, integrated circuits have been progressively improved without any startling innovations: in this type of research, IBM's thirty or so research laboratories throughout the world together spend £1300 million per year.

In fact, several dozen on-going IBM research projects roughly correlate with the Japanese efforts in the fifth-generation programme (there is, for instance, much work devoted to parallel processing). At the IBM Essonnes factory in France, 15,000 different kinds of chips are made, totalling up to 20 million chips every year, with about 10 per cent of the Essonnes output finding its way into IBM's most powerful computers, the 308X series. One of the 308X plants is in Japan, with the others in France and the US. In the next generation of computers, IBM are likely to retain many 308X features, including water cooling. With these types of on-going projects, we should be wary of assuming that the Japanese computer industry will be dominant by the end of the decade.

Another US initiative, taken as equivalent to what is recommended by Alvey (see below), is a $250 million Department of Defence software initiative built around Ada (reported in *Computing,* 25/11/82). This is part of a project in which $157 has already been allocated to the development of high-speed integrated circuits. If an effort is made to boost knowledge-based systems and man/machine interfaces, the investment could add up to about $1 billion.

The aim is that the software work will be contracted out to the private sector. There will be attention to R & D and to products already on the market or under development. The Department of Defence is to set up a national institute of software engineering with a brief to advance the progress of software technology. Efforts will also be made to sponsor live projects, involving new software technologies, within user departments. We may expect much of this work to be stimulated by awareness of the intentions behind the Japanese fifth-generation programme.

THE ALVEY REPORT

The Alvey Report (about 80 pages long) was published in September/October 1982 as a direct response to Japanese fifth-generation plans. (The various Japanese programmes are seen as 'a major competitive threat'.) The Report identifies four key technical areas in which major advances are required for the implementation of an Advanced Information Technology (AIT) programme:

— software engineering;

— man/machine interface (MMI);

— intelligent knowledge-based systems (IKBS);

— very large-scale integration (VLSI).

In the *Executive Summary* (Section 2), specific practical measures are proposed for the development of information technology in Britain. These recommendations include:

— investment of £350 million over five years, with Government providing three-quarters of the cost and industry providing the remainder (and also the 'much larger sums needed to translate the results of the programme into marketable products');

— collaborative effort between industry, the academic sector and other research organisations to get the best value from Government support;

— investment by Government of £57 million to support research and training in academic institutions, with dissemination of results 90 per cent funded by Government;

— an effective doubling of UK effort in the four enabling technologies: software engineering, MMI, IDBS and VLSI;

— participation of foreign multinationals in the UK effort, only where they can contribute a particular asset, where their involvement will benefit UK industry as a whole, and where it is guaranteed that valuable technical information will not leak from the UK;

— establishment of a new Directorate, within the Department of Industry, charged with implementing the programme. SERC and the Ministry of Defence should also be involved in the control of the programme and should provide some of the Government funding;

— early initiation of the programme.

The Case for the Programme (Section 3) is argued on the basis of five main propositions:

— on current trends, the UK share of the growing world IT market will diminish;

— to reverse these trends, it is necessary to have competitive levels of achievement in certain fundamental enabling technologies;

— the enabling technologies can be identified;

— a strong domestic capability in these technologies is required ('we cannot depend upon other countries supplying them');

— the necessary national collaborative effort requires Government backing.

Individual companies will be expected to exploit the results of the programme (whether or not they have been involved in its implementation), applying commercial judgments on market opportunities. It is emphasised that the level of Government support will render the results of the programme public property 'which can be made generally available for exploitation by British industry'. The potentially stimulating effect of the programme on small companies is seen as one of its major attractions. The proposed UK programme is represented as independent of the current ESPRIT proposals from the European Commission, though a collaborative UK programme 'would assist in feeding in the UK input to any EEC programme'. The French, for example, have embarked upon their own national IT programme, independent of Esprit.

Section 4 *(Technical Content and Targets)* explores an approach to the four identified enabling technologies: software engineering, MMI, IKBS and VLSI. It is suggested that a communication network be established to connect the organisations that will need to cooperate in developing these inter-dependent technologies. The importance, for software engineering, of developing Information Systems Factories (ISFs) is emphasised, and a development strategy for each of the enabling technologies is described in some detail (Section 4, occupying 38 pages, represents about half of the total report). Specific topics are discussed and development time-scales are defined.

In Section 5 *(Cost and Funding),* the proposed distribution of Government funding over the various elements in the programme (software engineering, VLSI, CAD, MMI, IKBS, communications, demonstrators and education) is tabulated for a five-year period (total cost: £352 million). It is expected that Government will fund the major share of the programme but that industry will need to raise 'the much larger funds needed to translate the results of the programme into marketable products'. Proposed academic investment (total: £56 million) is also shown distributed over the various programme elements.

Section 6 *(Management of the Programme)* explores the character of the proposed Directorate. A Director, with proper authority within the Department of Industry, will report to a Board which would serve as a steering committee. Assistant Directors are envisaged who would need to be expert authorities in their respective technical areas. The main task of the Directorate would be to ensure that the programme was effectively implemented, its targets met to the agreed timescale. It will award contracts, monitor projects, disseminate programme results, explore the question of Industrial Property Rights (IPR), etc.

Section 7 *(Human Resources)* explores the provision of the skilled manpower essential to the implementation of the programme. The Directorate will monitor the manpower requirements and, by means of recruitment and training, ensure that they are met. It is emphasised that the need to train personnel varies from one technical sector to another: there are, for example, few active participants in the UK in the IDBS area, though Britain has an excellent reputation for research in computer science. An IT Fellowship, a dispersed national institute, is proposed as a means of exploiting existing expertise. Action is also recommended in schools and other educational organisations.

Section 8 *(Summary of Recommendations)* lists proposals as ten discrete paragraphs. These identify such requirements as: the need for a national, Government-backed, collaborative effort; research in the enabling technologies; proportions of government and industry funding; identification of property rights; the need for a Directorate; and the timescale of the programme. It is concluded that 'the programme should be implemented immediately to safeguard the future competitiveness of the UK IT industry'.

REACTION TO ALVEY

General

One initial reaction to the Alvey Report was to contrast its recommendations with those of another report published ten years ago. In 1973 a *Report on Artificial Intelligence,* written by James Lighthill and issued by the then Science Research Council (SRC), argued that AI research cost too much and was unlikely to contribute to short-term commercial benefit. Alex d'Agapeyeff (and other observers) have noted that after the Lighthill report appeared, and until very recently, the SRC failed to fund any significant AI projects. We now know that artificial intelligence will be a key element in fifth-generation systems. Following Lighthill, funding was virtually abandoned in the UK, and AI work in such places as Edinburgh, Imperial College and Essex University continued despite, rather than encouraged by, official attitudes. More than one commentator has suggested that the Lighthill report has a lot to answer for.

The Alvey about-face on Lighthill, recommending expenditure of millions of pounds on knowledge-based systems, is not universally welcomed among UK pundits. Darrel Ince, for example, at the OU Institute of Mathematics, refers to the proposed scheme as a 'massive gamble', pointing to controversy over the performance of expert systems. For instance, with the AM expert system, long regarded as a classic in knowledge-based research, seeming discrepancies have emerged between theoretical predictions and actual performance. Further, 'there is little quantitative evidence of the success of knowledge-based systems in an industrial environment' *(Guardian,* 2/12/82).

More generally, reaction to the Alvey Report has been favourable, though many doubts have been expressed about when the present UK Government will readily enter into the large-scale financial commitment proposed. Various observers have predicted that the Government will never go along with the proposals. One leading company director (unnamed) is reported as saying that the 'proposals don't stand a dog's chance'. Other observers have suggested that the Government will try to obtain a larger proportion of the recommended funding from the private sector. Thus Tim Webb, national officer of ASTMS, declared that 'the Government is committed to giving support to IT, but they'll try and get a bigger input from the private sector, probably in 50-50 proportions.' In similar vein, John Garrett, Labour MP, predicted that the Government 'will try to lay as much of the funding as possible on private industry'.

Computer Industry Reaction

The computer industry has broadly supported the proposals of the Alvey Report although there is some significant dissent to record. Pearson (in *Computer Weekly,* 11/11/82) suggests that the 'consensus view is that Alvey is generally right, save for the obligatory quibblings about detail and emphasis'. Mark Dowson, a director of Imperial College Software Technology, is quoted: 'I have almost no reservations in welcoming the report . . .' At the same time, joined by Peter Thomas, marketing director of Pactel and president of the Computing Services Association, Dowson is concerned at the training emphasis. Academic training is seen as having a long lead time: there should be more emphasis on industrial training to develop the skills of existing practitioners (Thomas: 'Alvey's emphasis is more on computer science graduates: it takes years for someone to go through the system, and we need an early start'). David Rodway, technical director of SPL, suggested that 'we should have started this programme five years ago'.

Some observers consider that the funding philosophy (Section 5 in the Report) is unconvincing. Thus Professor Frank Sumner,

Manchester University, commented: 'It seems they have plucked the figures out of the air; it's one of the problems of having to deal with the Government. But only about £50 million of the total is properly worked out' (quoted by Pearson, 1982). Doug Eyeions, general secretary of CSA, has observed that 'it's a political football at the moment to fund new technology'.

Various software houses – Scicon, Logica, Systems Programmers, Systems Designers, Software Sciences, Pactel and Imperial Software Technology – expressed doubts about drafts of the Alvey Report, and resolved to publish their own proposals (reported in *Computing*, 7/10/82). One member of the group noted that 'we were all invited to contribute to the Alvey Report but subsequently became worried that our views were not represented . . . Although we are in agreement with the general thrust of the drafts of the report . . . they fall severely short on some issues . . .'. The group questioned the export of software engineering environments (software tools 'should be retained to create wealth'), and one member warned that UK software engineers should not be sent to Japan just to be pumped for two years. Bird (1982) reports some of the group's reservations about elements in the Alvey Report (for instance, the role of Unix may be over-emphasised).

Iann Barron, of Inmos and a member of the Alvey committee, has expressed doubts about assuming that PROLOG is the best 'kernel language' for fifth generation ('we should be reaching out for a language that is not currently within our grasp . . .'). Moreover, he suggests that the UK needs a *commercial* strategy on fifth-generation developments, and the Alvey proposals relate mainly to research (Barron: 'If we are going to have a fifth-generation programme we need lots more than just a research project: we need to find out how to sell that technology in the world'). In a similar spirit, Robb Wilmot, ICL managing director, declared that the Alvey committee 'did what they were asked to do, but the problem is much bigger than they were asked to tackle'.

Some criticism has been directed at Alvey's attempt to convey the need for capital investment on a grand scale. Hedley Voysey, referring to software engineering, talks of the 'gravest deficiency' in the Alvey Report resting 'on the brief treatment accorded to the reasons which are supporting the thesis'. And he sees as the other deficiency the idea that the proposed Directorate could work out implementations through mixed academic and industrial agents *(Computing,* 13/1/83).

David Fairbairn, Director of the National Computing Centre, observes that similarity between the Alvey focus of interest and the Japanese Fifth Generation proposals is not entirely coincidental: there is 'some consensus of what is important in the development of information technology'. He notes that the Report does not select 'the elements of the programme which are most appropriate for concentration of UK talents and energy'. Further, 'it is to be hoped that the case made by the Alvey Report for a concerted UK effort is heeded and that a substantial programme is launched with the least possible delay'. This, Mr Fairbairn observes, 'requires the committed support of both Government and the industry'.

On 9th February 1983, a report (produced by a team drawn from the 'sunrise industry' sectors of the National Economic Development Council) was published, urging the Government to accept the recommendations of the Alvey Report if Britain is to remain competitive in electronics. The NEDC report refers to 'the unprecedented willingness of companies to cooperate with each other' in Alvey-type research, and emphasises that without an implementation of Alvey the UK effort in the information technology field will remain fragmented ('The UK would then have to rely heavily on overseas sources, whose accessibility is subject to political factors, for essential enabling technologies . . . This would put the UK in an intolerable position of strategic weakness').

The NEDC team, representing both management and unions, urges the need for a focus on business objectives rather than on technological objectives. Funding should not be diverted from existing Government programmes, and the Alvey scheme should be implemented in alignment with the EEC's Esprit microelectronics programme.

Government Reaction

The Government's initial reaction to Alvey was one of measured silence. An editorial in *Computer Weekly* (14/10/82) observes that the day after the Report was issued, Industry Secretary Patrick Jenkin and Employment Secretary Norman Tebbit addressed the

Conservative Computer Forum in Brighton. Jenkin pointed out that since it came to office the Government had more than doubled expenditure on new technology. Further, £1 billion would be spent in the next three years under the terms of the Science and Technology Acts. However, no mention was made of Alvey. The CW editorial commented that it was 'no sure thing' that the Alvey proposals would be accepted by the Government ('We hope that the quiet response to the report is a sign that many people are reflecting deeply on its implications . . . We await with interest to see how quickly the government accepts the challenge to back its own vision of the future').

The *Europa Report* (15/11/82) noted that 'one by one the big guns of industry and the universities are putting their weight' behind the Alvey proposals, and added that the only people 'resisting and ignoring the report are the Department of Industry, sponsors of the report, and the Treasury . . .'. No reference was made to the Alvey Report in the Chancellor's Autumn statement ('Politicians of all persuasions are, we know, very good at talking but far less good at actually doing things'). Charles Read, one of the members of the Alvey committee, has expressed doubt on the Government's willingness to adopt the Alvey proposals *(Computer Weekly,* 30/9/82). Read suggested that the lesson of Japanese funding for the fifth-generation project would be difficult for the current government to swallow. Moreover, he sees the UK as lacking the proper infrastructure for a collaborative effort similar to that of the Japanese ('We cannot hope to run down the infrastructure of education the way we are doing and hope to survive').

Kevin Cahill records *(Computer Weekly,* 11/11/82) that some observers see the Alvey Report as politically naive, noting that Kenneth Baker, Information Technology Minister, is understood to have favoured a formal link with Japan on a fifth-generation programme. (Professor Moto-oko, chairman of the Japanese project expressed concern at the Pergamon Infotech Conference that so far no country or company had gone into formal collaboration with Japan, a matter of some concern to the Japanese.) Baker is also thought to have made clear that Alvey should have indicated the sources of proposed financial investment. And it was also argued, at a recent Pitcom (Parliamentary Information Technology Committee Meeting), that Alvey was wrong to emphasise the scale of the Japanese threat. A number of Pitcom members suggested that perhaps the Government would try to ignore the Alvey proposals. Philip Hughes, chairman of Logica and a member of the committee, told the Pitcom meeting that there had been no response to the Alvey proposals from the Department of Industry, the Treasury or Parliament.

By mid-November 1982 it was, however, reported that the Government was set to give its support to the recommendations of the Alvey Report. Soon after Christmas, it was predicted, a firm decision would be made, and Kenneth Baker was suggesting that the ministries involved – including the Department of Industry, the Department of Education, and the Ministry of Defence – would find a substantial part of the £350 million estimated cost. Baker was also quoted (in *Computing,* 18/11/82) as saying that 'I am convinced that the world is going to come out of the recession not as a result of demand push but as a result of technology push'. In early-1983 there were reports (eg in *Infomatics,* February 1983) that the UK Department of Industry had approved the £350 million expenditure (over five years) recommended in the Alvey Report, and that full Government approval would follow after consultation with other Departments.

SUMMARY

The response to the Japanese fifth-generation plans is profiled with attention to attitudes in the US, the UK and elsewhere. It is suggested that the Japanese project may not be quite the cataclysm that many pundits seem keen to depict. An indication is given of the scale of IBM activities in areas that are relevant to fifth-generation development.

The main UK response to fifth-generation plans, the setting up of the Alvey committee (and its subsequent Report), is profiled, and a brief indication provided of the response of the computer industry and the Government to the Report's proposals. The seeming lack of Government interest in the Alvey Report is noted, though Kenneth Baker is seen to have made optimistic noises.

The response to fifth-generation plans in general and to the Alvey Report in particular will be best judged when some time has passed, and with hindsight. In the months and years ahead, the scale of investment in fifth-generation and the resulting products will be the best indication of how Britain responded to the international challenge.

7 The Future

GENERAL

Much of this book is about the future. Fifth-generation computers are not yet with us, though many of the contributing technologies are well established. The new systems will need to operate faster and with a higher degree of circuit integration. It has been suggested (eg in *The Guardian*, 27/8/80) that new lithographic methods could become sufficiently precise to build transistors as small as biological molecules in cellular matter. Such microchips 'with lines less than half a micron wide (a micron is a thousandth of a millimetre), might spontaneously reorganise their own functions, might provide a physics laboratory on a single chip, or microscopic electronic aids knitted to the human neural system'. By the end of the decade, silicon chips could have evolved to the point where a single chip could contain more than one million components. Such chips will be a hundred times denser than most of today's products, and we would be able to construct even a relatively sophisticated computer system (eg the IBM 370) on a single sliver of silicon. Professor K T Hung of Carnegie Mellon University has considered the possibility of a processor that would handle around 2000 million operations per second. For such a high level of performance, multiple arithmetic units working in parallel would be necessary, akin to the columnar structures in the human neocortex. And the new processors would not need to rely upon silicon. We have briefly indicated the work with gallium arsenide and Josephson junctions, and other possibilities are emerging.

SYNERGETICS

Such existing supercomputers as the Cray-1 and the Cyber 205 can perform more than 100 million operations per second, allowing the creation of highly accurate three-dimensional simulations for such purposes as weather forecasting and geological prospecting. Mathematical models have been constructed on some large computers to stimulate arrays of microelectronic devices which are 'partly isolated' from each other. This means that, in particular circumstances, additional communication channels can be deliberately opened between the devices over and above the conventional wired-in connections. Communication is facilitated at this level by various esoteric physical effects (eg charge spill-over following lowering of the atomic tunnelling barriers). This work, being conducted at Warwick University (UK), may pave the way for structuring highly flexible data processing arrays, designs capable of rearranging an original electrical configuration.

Research into *synergetics,* a recently-formed science looking at, amongst other things, how certain types of system can spontaneously restructure themselves, is yielding theoretical principles that may be relevant to the computers of the future. Scientists have found that some of the mathematical equations used to model such self-organising behaviour resemble equations used to define the behaviour of the partially-isolated arrays modelled by computer. Some information-processing functions of the brain have been interpreted in terms of synergetic neural networks in the cerebral cortex. In short, a practical computer technology can be envisaged which will be able to duplicate some of the most refined elements in the human, a manifest requirement in fifth-generation computers that will be expected to reason, recognise patterns and carry out other high-level cognitive tasks.

It has already been found that certain types of logic arrays can reorganise themselves automatically when damage occurs to components. This ability, analogous to the biological brain's facility for switching functions to other neural circuits when necessary, is clearly relevant to automatic fault-diagnosis, fault tolerance, and system reliability. Synergetic behaviour requires that many processes occur simultaneously: a manifest feature of normal brain working, and a much-quoted characteristic of fifth-generation computer systems.

THE BIOCHIP

Some of this work relates to the design of *biochips,* important both to medicine and to the future of computing. Biochips, constructed out of organic materials, will be able to operate at the molecular level and in three-dimensional arrays. They will therefore allow for a high level of circuit integration with a massive increase in circuit complexity (by contrast, silicon-chip circuits are laid out on two-dimensional wafers). At the same time, some biochips will exploit the characteristics of silicon.

EMV Associates, in Rockville, Maryland, is currently exploring the possibility of combining organic switching molecules and computer design. One possibility is to replace conventional computer silicon with thin layers of organic molecules which will handle electronics as does a conventional computer. It may become possible to trigger the growth of a protein film in a highly structured way to grow logic gates at particular points: in such a fashion, genetic engineering could be enlisted to grow computers. This possibility should not surprise us. After all, biological genes have generated computers for many millions of years: namely, the biological brains in thousands of animal species.

Today working biochips are called chemical and ion selective field effect transistors (ChemFETs and ISFETs). These devices are able to detect the presence of specific chemical substances in a liquid and communicate the concentration as an electrical signal: a simple type of molecule can be precisely determined against a background of other substances. For example, the active region of a ChemFET may be a small portion of silicon chip bathed in a solution and enclosed in a plastic membrane exposed to the outside world. The membrane is impregnated with an enzyme which reacts with the molecule to be detected.

The development of biochips that have both chemical and electrical features extends further the similarity between computer elements and brain cells. We have known for a long time that the behaviour of neurons is more than a purely electrical affair. Messages are conveyed through the brain and around the rest of the organism by means of hormones as well as by electrical signals. Circulating hormones can be used to stimulate the growth of neuron dendrites – to make new connections, to build up fresh 'hard-wired' programs. The arrival of a nerve impulse at a synapse stimulates the nerve to release a chemical which diffuses through the cellular membrane to arrive at the second. The subsequent depolarisation of the cell membrane causes an impulse in the second nerve.

Each individual cell responds according to the relationship between the internal composition of the cell and the medium at the other side of a critical membrane. The disposition of ions (eg of such elements as sodium and chloride) governs the electrical behaviour of the cell, and so controls the transmission of information through the system. In a similar way, the field-effect transistors do not respond to electrical current from a conventional power source, as do computer circuits, but rely on the electrical potential created by selected ions. ISFETs are analogous to biological neurons in their reliance on ions for an energy source, and in using a membrane to control the passage of ions.

The first biochip was patented in 1974 by Arieh Aviram and Philip Seiden (both of IBM) and Mark Ratner (of New York University). However, IBM reckoned that the biochip was a non-starter and focused its chip research elsewhere. Others have been more enthusiastic. John Elkington, associate editor of *Biotechnology Bulletin*, has quoted (in *The Guardian*, 20/1/83) James McAlear's hopes for molecular electronics. Here the 3-dimensional protein lattice would open up the possibility of 3-dimensional circuits, increased speeds, reduced energy consumption, and ultra-miniaturisation that can reach a million billion elements per cubic centimetre'. Furthermore, 'on this scale, all the memory elements of every computer manufactured to this day could be contained in a cube one centimetre on a side'.

McAlear's company, Gentronix, now holding two patents in this area, has recently signed an agreement with the Tokyo-based company, Mitsui, to encourage Japanese investment in biochip technology.

One of the patents covers the use of a protein with a resist material (polymethyl methacrylate) that can be exposed with an electron beam. A developer can remove the exposed material, allowing the protein to support subsequent circuitry layers. The second patent deals with the production of an 'oriented protein monolayer', in which molecules line up in an electric field. Following exposure and development, the protein circuitry is oriented in the direction of the field. Such ideas may be seen as initial steps on the road to biological computers. Kevin Ulmer, of Genex, sees the ultimate scenario as the development of 'a complete genetic code for the computer that would function as a virus does, but instead of producing more virus, it would assemble a fully operational computer inside a cell' (quoted by Elkington, 1983).

The development of the biochip as an element in computer systems has been seen by some observers as belonging to mainstream fifth-generation research. Others have depicted the biochip as a *sixth*-generation concern.

ROBOTICS

There can be little doubt that robots will become more competent, more flexible and more intelligent, and that this development will be intimately linked to progress in fifth-generation research. Two recent articles in *Computer Design* (Gupta, 1982; Goshorn, 1982) indicate how robots are acquiring more flexible microprocessor-based intelligence. Ideally, for example, a robot requires a microcontroller per axis, with *on-board* intelligence the norm: trailing cables are a disadvantage, particularly with mobile systems.

Enhanced robot intelligence will emerge in conjunction with more user-friendly man/machine interfaces. (You'll be able to speak to your industrial or domestic robot to tell it what to do.) And applications will become more impressive. For example, a recently-announced robot vision system, from Object Recognition Systems Inc, enables robots to retrieve parts that are jumbled randomly in a box or bin (described in *Electronics*, 30/11/82). The i-bot 1 system adds vision to an off-the-shelf robot arm. It is trained by being shown the objects it will encounter: patterns are stored to facilitate later comparisons in the operating environment.

The scope of modern robotics research is indicated by the range of papers presented to (for example) the Twelfth International Symposium on Industrial Robotics (9th-11th June 1982, Paris). Here, new or enhanced applications were described for forging, assembling, arc-welding, etc. There were even papers dealing with automatic chocolate decoration and automatic sheep shearing!

One paper, of particular relevance to the development of an intelligence man/machine interface, focuses on 'a pragmatic interpreter of a task-oriented subset of natural language for robotic purposes' (see Evrard et al). Such a facility would enable a robot to understand English, French, Japanese, etc.

It is easy to envisage a situation in which robots could understand spoken instructions and behave in an intelligent fashion. We have already seen a proliferation of intelligent robots in films and fiction, and a few highly expensive domestic robots have been built. In 1977, Quasar Industries built a robot that could mop floors, mow lawns and do simple cooking. Similarly, the Reckitt industrial robot, first launched in the late-seventies could scrub and polish floors, dust desks and other furniture, sweep and vacuum, and remove excess water. And in 1982 Mitsubishi announced a robot that was dexterous enough to light a cigarette and pick up a telephone. Perhaps most remarkably, in late-1982 we heard about Cubot, an American robot which is able – using its mechanical fingers, camera eye and computer brain – to solve any scrambled Rubik's cube in less than four minutes! In the years to come, robots allied to fifth-generation computer power will be useful, but perhaps daunting, creatures.

SUMMARY AND CONCLUSION

This chapter has sketched developments in synergetics, biochips and robotics. The few illustrations indicate that the future will be shaped by progress in systems techniques, circuit developments (leading to faster and more highly integrated configurations), and applications (where, for example, robots will be able to understand English). There is even the possibility that electrical pulses will be able to move faster than light: Anthony Tucker has reported (in *The Guardian,* 6/1/83) on work at Sussex University that could make existing computer systems 'seem like semaphore' (see also 'The Time Machinery', by Dr Terry Clark, head of the cryogenic studies team at the University of Sussex, in *Guardian* 'Futures' 6/1/83). In *Scientific American* (February 1983), Eitan Abraham et al describe how a computer based on beams of light rather than on electric currents might be capable of a trillion operations per second. Already, an optical analogue of the transistor has been built.

Fifth-generation computer systems may not emerge exactly in the form currently defined by the research planners. It may prove necessary to shift emphasis, to trim ambitions. New-generation systems will certainly emerge – possibly, as IBM seems to imagine, by the progressive enhancement of existing configurations – but they may differ in important aspects from the concepts currently being framed by the Japanese specialists. For example, the question of inference may prove intractable, particularly with the need to model fuzzy modes of reasoning. The levels of inference that may be achieved may be too primitive to support the artificial intelligence that is at the heart of the fifth-generation concept. Piecemeal development of expert systems, focused on particular promising specialist domains, may be the best that can be hoped for, at least by the fifth-generation prototype target year of 1991.

It is easy to point to the difficulties that face development of true fifth-generation systems (as defined in the Japanese research projects). The programme is, after all, the most ambitious that the computer industry has seen. It is inevitable that there will be a fifth generation of computers, and sixth, and a seventh . . . And it is certain that the current fifth-generation programme will influence directly the shape of future computers. But, as has been the case with all the earlier computer generations, it will be easiest to recognise fifth-generation computers when they have finally emerged, when they are successfully performing in the world.

APPENDIX 1
Bibliography

CHAPTER 1

Beresford R, GaAs Symposium Struts Useful Stuff, *Electronics,* 3/11/82, p 49

Beresford R, Devices Meeting Probes the Limits of Semiconductors and Circuitry, *Electronics,* 15/12/82, pp 138-145

Bursky D, New Supercomputer, Multiple-Layer ICs Among Goals in Japan, *Electronic Design,* 29/4/82, pp 40-41

Cahill K, Japan Looks to the Future, *Data Processing,* September 1982, pp 28-31

Evanczuk S, Microsystems (in Annual Technology Update), *Electronics,* 20/10/82, pp 172-176

Lavington S H, *A History of Manchester Computers,* NCC Publications, 1975

Malik R, Walking, Talking Computers are on the Way, *Financial Guardian,* 7/7/82

Marsh P, The Race for the Thinking Machine, *New Scientist,* 8/7/82, pp 85-87

Michie D, Turing and the Origins of the Computer, *New Scientist,* 21/2/80, pp 580-583

Nogami M, Hirachi Y and Ohta K, Present State of Microwave GaAs Devices, *Microelectronics Journal,* volume 13, number 3, 1982, pp 29-43

Peltu M, *Introducing Computers,* NCC Publications, 1983

Rubinfeld P I, Two-Chip Supermicroprocessor Outperforms PDP-11 Minicomputers, *Electronics,* 15/12/82, pp 131-136

Spennewyn D, Where Super Systems Go, *Computing,* 28/10/82, p 32

Supercomputer Battle Hots Up, *Infomatics,* December 1982, p 10

Treleaven P C and Lima I G, Japan's Fifth-Generation Computer Systems, *Computer,* August 1982, pp 79-88

CHAPTER 2

Bibliographic note: the first 18 listed papers together comprise the *Proceedings of the International Conference on Fifth-Generation Computer Systems,* 19-22 October 1981, published by the Japan Information Processing Development Centre (JIPDEC). The other citations in this section appear alphabetically as usual.

Papers from Conference Proceedings

Moto-oka et al, Challenge for Knowledge Information Processing Systems, Keynote Speech

Karatsu H, What is Required of the Fifth-Generation Computer – Social Needs and Its Impact

Fuchi K, Aiming for Knowledge Information Processing Systems

Aiso H, Fifth-Generation Architecture

Furukawa K et al, Problem-Solving and Inference Mechanisms

Suwa M, Knowledge Base Mechanisms

Tanaka H et al, Intelligent Man/Machine Interface

Yokoi T et al, Logic Programming and a Dedicated High-Performance Personal Computer

Uchida S et al, New Architectures for Inference Mechanisms

Amamiya M et al, New Architecture for Knowledge Base Mechanisms

Sakamura K et al, VLSI and System Architecture – The Development of System 5G

Tanaka H et al, The Preliminary Research on Data Flow Machine and Data Base Machine as the Basic Architecture of Fifth-Generation Computer Systems

Feigenbaum E A, Innovation in Symbol Manipulation in the Fifth-Generation Computer Systems

Bibel W, Logical Program Synthesis

Kahn G, The Scope of Symbolic Computation

McCormick B H et al, A Cognitive Architecture for Computer Vision

Treleaven P C, Fifth-Generation Computer Architecture Analysis

Allen G, Algorithms, Architecture and Technology

Other References

Amamiya M, Valid – A High-Level Functional Language for Data Flow Machines, *Research Reports in Japan,* JIPDEC, Fall 1981, pp 222-238

Cahill K, Japan Looks to the Future, The Organisation and Technology of the Japanese Computer Industry, *Data Processing,* September 1982, pp 28-31

Fawcett S, Occam Talks in Parallel Lines, *Computing,* 2/12/82, p 19

Fifth-Generation Computers, *JIPDEC Report,* Summer 1980, 42 pp

Goto S, DURAL: A Modal Extension of Prolog, *Research Reports in Japan,* JIPDEC, Fall 1981, pp 289-294

Japanese Goal – To Kill Off Current Languages, *Computer Weekly,* 7/10/82, p 12

Jones K, Fifth-Generation MIT Computers Bring Parallel Architectures to US, *Mini-Micro Systems,* September 1982, pp 103-111

Manuel T, Computers and Peripherals, *Electronics,* 20/10/82, pp 188-196

Marsh P, The Race for the Thinking Machine, *New Scientist,* 8/7/82, pp 85-87

Mercer A and Vincent G, Controllers Built Using Function-to-Function Architecture, *Industrial Robot,* December 1982, pp 228-232

Outline of Research and Development Plans for Fifth-Generation Computer Systems, ICOT (Institute for New Generation Computer Technology), May 1982, 23 pp

Software Conference Stresses Cooperation, is Short on Technology, *Electronic Design,* 11/11/82, pp 61E-66E

Sowa M and Murata T, A Data Flow Computer Architecture with Program and Token Memories, *IEEE Transactions on Computers,* volume C-31, Number 9, September 1982, pp 820-824

Special Report on Japan, *Computing,* 29/7/82, pp 13-19, includes:
Fifth-Generation: A Thorny Co-operation Task
Three Steps Towards Up-to-Date Technology
Miti's Rising Vision
Reaping Fruits of 5 Years' Chip Research
A Bird? A Plane? No, It's Super Kit
Hello, This is Your Bank (on pattern recognition)

Treleaven P C and Lima I G, Japan's Fifth-Generation Computer Systems, *Computer,* August 1982, pp 79-88

CHAPTER 3

Allen R B, Cognitive Factors in Human Interaction with Computers, *Behaviour and Information Technology,* volume 1, number 3, 1982, pp 257-278

Allport D A, Patterns and Actions: Cognitive Mechanisms are Content-Specific, in Guy Claxton (ed), *Cognitive Psychology: New Directions,* Routledge and Kegan Paul, 1980

Barr A and Feigenbaum E (eds), *The Handbook of Artificial Intelligence,* volumes 1 and 2, Pitman, 1981 and 1982

Bobrow D G (ed), *Artificial Intelligence,* special issue on non-monotonic logic, 13 (1, 2), 1980

Boden M, *Artificial Intelligence and Natural Man,* Harvester Press, 1977

Bond A, Change in Rules for Intelligence, *Computing,* 5/3/81, pp 18-19

Burkitt A, How Donald Michie Was Flipped Off His Feet by AI, *Computing,* 15/7/82, pp 32-33

Clark H H and Clark E V, *Psychology and Language: An Introduction to Psycholinguistics,* Harcourt Brace Jovanovich, New York, 1977

Cohen P R and Feigenbaum E (eds), *The Handbook of Artificial Intelligence,* volume 3, 1982

Computers that Learn Could Lead to Disaster, *New Scientist,* 17/1/80, p 160

Ernst G and Newell A, *GPS: A Case Study in Generality and Problem Solving,* Academic Press, New York, 1969

Hello, This is Your Bank, in special report, *Computing,* 29/7/82, p 20

Hunt E, What kind of a Computer is Man? *Cognitive Psychology,* volume 2, 1971, pp 57-98

Klir J and Valach M, *Cybernetic Modelling,* Iliffe Books, London, 1965

Lawson V (ed), *Practical Experience of Machine Translation,* Conference Proceedings, London, 5-6/11/81

Lee G et al, Artificial Intelligence, History and Knowledge Representation, *Computers and the Humanities,* September 1982, pp 25-34

Mason B, Intelligence Tests for Computers? *Practical Computer World,* December 1982, pp 134-137

Matheson W, The Brain and the Machine, *Personal Computing,* April 1978, pp 37-45

Michie D, P-KP4; Expert System to Human Being Conceptual Checkmate of Dark Ingenuity, *Computing,* 17/7/80

Miller G A, The Magic Number Seven, Plus or Minus Two, *Psychological Review,* volume 63, 1956, pp 81-97

Miller G A and Johnson-Laird P N, *Language and Perception,* Cambridge University Press, 1976

Minsky M, A Framework for Representing Knowledge, in Haugeland (ed), *Mind Design: Philosophy, Psychology, Artificial Intelligence,* Bradford Books, 1980

Neisser U, *Cognitive Psychology,* Appleton-Century-Crofts, New York, 1967

Newell A et al, Elements of a Theory of Human Problem Solving, *Psychological Review,* volume 65, 1958, pp 151-166

Newell et al, Report on a General Problem Solving Program, *Proceedings of the International Conference on Information Processing,* Paris, Unesco House, 1959

Newell A et al, Empirical Explanations with the Logic Theory Machines: A Case Study in Heuristics, in E A Feigenbaum and J Feldman (eds) *Computers and Thought,* McGraw-Hill, New York, 1963

Newell A and Simon H A, *Human Problem Solving,* Prentice-Hall, Englewood Cliffs, N. J., 1972

Orme M, Searching for the Key to AI, *Infomatics,* August 1982, pp 24-27

Reitman J S, Information Processing Model of STM in D A Norman (ed), *Models of Human Memory,* Academic Press, London and New York, 1970

Robinson J A, A Machine-Oriented Logic Based on the Resolution Principle, *Journal of the ACM,* 12, 1965, pp 23-41

Scraggs G W, Answering Questions About Processes, in D A Norman and D E Rumelhart (eds), *Exploration in Cognition,* W H Freeman, San Francisco, 1975

Sloman, A, *The Computer Revolution in Philosophy,* Harvester Press, 1978

Travis A J B, An Aid to Pattern Recognition, *Computer Journal,* volume 25, number 1, 1982, pp 37-44

Waltz D. L, Artificial Intelligence, *Scientific American,* October 1982, pp 101-122

Wang H, Towards Mechanical Mathematics, *IBM Journal of Research and Development,* 4, 1960, pp 2-22

Weisstein N, Beyond the Yellow Volkswagen Detector and the Grandmother Cell: A General Strategy for the Exploration of Operations in Human Pattern Recognition, in R L Solso (ed), *Contemporary Issues in Cognitive Psychology: the Loyola Symposium,* Winston/Wiley, Washington, 1973

Whitehead A N and Russell B, *Principia Mathematica,* (2nd edition, volume 1), Cambridge University Press, 1925

Winograd T, Computer Memories: A Metaphor for Memory Organisation, in C Cofer (ed), *The Structure of Human Memory,* W H Freeman, San Francisco, 1975

CHAPTER 4

Addis T R, Expert Systems: An Evolution in Information Retrieval, *Information Technology: Research and Development,* number 1, 1982, pp 301-324

Barr A and Feigenbaum E A, *The Handbook of Artificial Intelligence,* volume 2, Pitman, 1982

Bennett B, Expert Replacement?, *Practical Computing,* December 1982, p 53

Bond A, Change in Rules for Intelligence, *Computing,* 5/3/81, pp 18-19

Changing Face of Micros, *Infomatics,* August 1982, p 3

Cole B C, Artificial Intelligence and the Personal Computer User, *Interface Age,* April 1981, pp 88-90

D'Agapeyeff A, *Expert Systems, Fifth Generation and UK Suppliers,* NCC Publications 1983

Duda R et al, Model Design in the PROSPECTOR Consultant System for Mineral Exploration, in D Michie (ed), *Expert Systems in the Microelectronics Age,* Edinburgh University Press, 1980

Expert Office Systems Get a Step Closer, *Computer Weekly,* 23/9/82, p 11

Fagan L M, *VM: Representing Time Dependent Relations in a Medical Setting,* Dissertation, Computer Science Department, Stanford University, USA, 1980

Fitter M J and Cruickshank P J, The Computer in the Consulting Room: A psychological Framework, *Behaviour and Information Technology,* volume 1, number 1, 1982, pp 81-92

Fox J, Computers Learn the Bedside Manner, *New Scientist,* 29/7/82, p 311-313

Gini G and Gini M, A Serial Model for Computer Assisted Medical Diagnosis, *International Journal of Biomedical Computing,* 11, 1980, pp 99-113

Hunter P, The Man With a Dedicated Approach to Expert Systems, *Computer Weekly,* 15/7/82, p 17

Parry R, DHSS Guinea Pig for Expert Systems, *Computer Weekly,* 6/1/83, p 1

Rogers W et al, Computer-Aided Medical Diagnosis: Literature Review, *International Journal of Biomedical Computing,* 10, 1979, pp 267-289

Shaket E, Fuzzy Semantics for a Natural-Like Language Defined Over a World of Blocks, *Artificial Intelligence, Memo 4,* University of California, 1976

Smith M F and Bowen J A, Knowledge and Experience-Based Systems for Analysis and Design of Microprocessor Applications Hardware, *Microprocessors and Microsystems,* December 1982, pp 515-518

Webster R, Expert Systems, *Personal Computer World,* January 1983, pp 118-119

Zadeh L A, Fuzzy Sets, *Information and Control,* 8, 1965, pp 338-353

CHAPTER 5

Agin G J, Computer Vision Systems for Industrial Inspection and Assembly, *Computer,* May 1980, pp 11-20

As Speech-Recognition Products Improve, Office Applications Appear, *Electronic Design,* 10/6/82, pp SS5-SS6

Bassak G, Phoneme-Based Speech Chip Needs Less Memory, *Electronics,* 3/7/80, pp 43-44

Boden M, *Artificial Intelligence and Natural Man,* Harvester Press 1977

Brightman T and Crook S, Exploring Practical Speech I/O, *Mini-Micro Systems,* May 1982, pp 291-305

Chan C and Lee M, Software Guides Designs for Speech Recognition, *Electronic Design,* 30/9/82, pp 143-147

Cohen P R and Feigenbaum E A, *The Handbook of Artificial Intelligence,* Volume 3, Pitman, 1982

Dixon J K, Pattern Recognition With Partly Missing Data, *IEEE Transactions on Systems, Man and Cybernetics,* October 1979, pp 617-621

Emerson S T, Listen: That Voice May Not Be Human, *Data Management,* August 1982, pp 18-19

Fields S W, Speech Synthesis to be Simple as CP/M, *Electronics,* 8/9/82, pp 49-50

Foss, L J, Voice Response Systems, *Data Management,* August 1982, pp 16-17

Hoff M E and Wallace L, Software Makes a Big Talker Out of the 2920 Microcomputer, *Electronics,* 31/1/80, pp 102-107

IBM Voice Synthesis Technology Gives Audio typing Unit Simulated speech Capabilities, *Software Digest,* 8/11/79, pp 3-4

Iversen W R, Military Has Its Eye on Speech, *Electronics,* 5/6/80, pp 93-94

Iversen R D et al, A Software Interface for speech Recognition, *Computer Design,* March 1982, pp 147-152

Jain R and Haynes S, Imprecision in Computer Vision, *Computer,* August 1982, pp 39-47

Jarvis J F, Visual Inspection Automation, *Computer,* May 1980, pp 32-38

Jarvis R A, A Computer Vision and Robotics Laboratory, *Computer,* June 1982, pp 8-22

Kaplan S J and Ferris D, Natural Language in the DP World, *Datamation,* August 1982, pp 114-120

Kennett D, Robot Vision System Can Recognise Human Faces in Three Seconds, *Computer Weekly,* 17-24/12/81, p 4

LeBoss B, Pair of Chips Synthesises Lifelike Speech, *Electronics,* 27/3/80, pp 39-40

LeBoss B, Speech I/O is Making Itself Heard, *Electronics*, 22/5/80, pp 95-105

Lineback J R, Voice Recognition Listens for Its Cue, *Electronics*, 13/1/83, pp 110-112

Linggard R and Marlow F J, Programmable, Digital Speech Synthesiser, *Computers and Digital Techniques*, October 1979, pp 191-196

Logica Defeats Continuous Speech Snags, *Computing*, 14/10/82, p 32

Manchester P, Getting Voice Response Into Working Order, *Computing*, 15/11/82, pp 50-51

McCormick B H et al, A Cognitive Architecture for Computer Vision, *Proceedings of the International Conference on Fifth-Generation Computer Systems*, 19-22 October 1981, JIPDEC

Miller F W, Talk It Over With your Computer, *Infosystems*, No. 8, 1978, pp 62-65

Myers W, Industry Begins to Use Visual Pattern Recognition, *Computer*, May 1980, pp 21-31

Onda H and Ohashi Y, Introduction of Visual Equipment to Inspection, *The Industrial Robot*, September 1979, pp 131-135

Researchers Make Gains in Computer Speech Recognition, *Canadian Data Systems*, May 1980, pp 86-87

S-100 Peripheral Card Converts Text Input into Natural-Sounding French Speech Output, *Electronics*, 13/1/83, pp 10E, 12E

Samuel D J, Talking Console Monitor Alerts Field Service, *Computer Design*, November 1981, pp 147-149

Scott B L, Voice Recognition Systems and Strategies, *Computer Design*, January 1983, pp 67-70

Silicon Speech, *Engineering*, November 1982, pp 793-796

Simons G L, *Robots in Industry*, NCC Publications, 1980

Tanaka H et al, Intelligent Man/Machine Interface, *Proceedings of the International Conference on Fifth Generation Computer Systems*, 19-22 October 1981, JIPDEC

Tennant H, Natural Language Processing and Small Systems, *Byte,* June 1978, pp 38-54

Thomas A F and Stout K J, Robot Vision, *Engineering,* May 1980, pp 533-537

TRS-80 Gets Voice Recognition, *Electronics,* 17/7/80, p 154

Vision and Speech Causes Sensation at Osaka, *FMS Update,* January 1983, p 1

Voice-Recognition Unit for Data Processing Can Handle 120 Words, *Electronics,* 13/4/78, pp 69-70

Weinrich, D W, Speech-Synthesis Chip Borrows Human Intonation, *Electronics,* 10/4/80, pp 113-118

Welch J R, Automatic Speech Recognition – Putting It to Work in Industry, *Computer,* May 1980, pp 65-73

Wickersham F et al, Bringing Speech to Low-Volume Products, *Mini-Micro Systems,* June 1982, pp 219-221

Wiggins R and Brantingham L, Three-Chip System Synthesises Human Speech, *Electronics,* 31/8/79, pp 109-116

Wilder J, Practical Pattern Recognition Approaches to Industrial Vision Problems, *Assembly Engineering,* December 1980, pp 12-15

Witkowski M, An Eye to the Future With Computer Vision, *Practical Computing,* July 1980, pp 90-98

Yachida M and Tsuji S, Industrial Computer Vision in Japan, *Computer,* May 1980, pp 50-63

CHAPTER 6

A Program for Advanced Information Technology. The Report of the Alvey Committee, September/October 1982

Bird J, Seven Critics Join to Challenge Alvey, *Computing,* 7/10/82, p 1

Bird J, Alvey 'Astray' Say Rival Group of 7, *Computing,* 14/10/82, p 14

Cahill K, Japanese Report Seen As 'Technological Mein Kampf', *Computer Weekly*, 15/7/82, p 5

Cahill K, Cold Feet on 5th Generation, *Computer Weekly*, 30/9/82, p 1

Cahill K, ICL to Wrap Up Its Fifth Generation in VME, *Computer Weekly*, 14/10/82, p 3

Debate, *Europa Report*, 15/11/82, p 1

Dinman, S B, The Fifth-Generation Gap, *Computer Design*, October 1982, p 11

DoI Hints at Alvey Cash, *Computing*, 18/11/82, p 1

Harmeleen M V, Fifth Generation Conference, *Data Processing*, September 1982, p 32

Hunter P, Fifth Generation Plans Not As Grand as Some Suppose Say Japanese, *Computer Weekly*, 29/7/82, p 1

IBM Rises to the Japanese Challenge, *New Scientist*, 29/7/82, p 304

Ince D, Making the Most of Intelligence, *The Guardian*, 2/12/82

Large P, The Need to Collaborate With Japan's Fifth Columnists, *The Guardian*, 13/5/82, p 15

Park M, What's It All About Alvey?, *Computer Talk*, 18/10/82, p 1

Pearson K, Political Cloud Over Alvey, *Computer Weekly*, 4/11/82, p 1

Pearson K, Thumbs Up for Alvey – But No Word from Govt, *Computer Weekly*, 11/11/82, p 7

Roberts G, UK Reply to Japanese Fifth Generation Project, *Microprocessors and Microsystems*, December 1982, p 543

Teaching DP's Value Rather Than Techniques, *Computing*, 4/11/82, pp 22-23

Voysey H, The Great Need to Invest on a Grand Scale, *Computing*, 13/1/82, p 15

What Alvey Means to the Dp Industry, *Computer Talk*, 18/10/82, p 4

Whither the Alvey Report?, *Computer Weekly*, 14/10/82

CHAPTER 7

Abraham E et al, The Optical Computer, *Scientific American*, February 1983, pp 63-71

Barker J, Now It's Smaller than Light, *Guardian*, 'Futures', 27/3/80

Clark T, The Time Machinery, *Guardian*, 'Futures', 6/1/83

Elkington J, Knockout Enzymes, *Guardian*, 'Futures', 20/1/83

Evrard F et al, A Pragmatic Interpreter of a Task-Oriented Subset of Natural Language for Robotic Purposes, *Proceedings of the Twelfth International Symposium on Industrial Robots*, 9th-11th June 1982, Paris, pp 531-540

Goshorn L A, A Single-Board Approach to Robotic Intelligence, *Computer Design*, November 1982, pp 193-201

Gupta P, Multiprocessing Improves Robotic Accuracy and Control, *Computer Design*, November 1982, pp 169-176

Iversen W R, Robot Picks Out of a Bin, *Electronics*, 30/11/82, p 50

Large P, After Silicon Has Had Its Chips, *Guardian*, 'Futures', 6/12/79

Tucker A, Signals That May Travel Faster than Light, *The Guardian*, 6/1/83

Yanchinski S, And Now – the Biochip, *New Scientist*, 14/1/82, p 68

Index

Index

215